DESIGNING
INTERFACE ANIMATION
MEANINGFUL MOTION FOR USER EXPERIENCE

Val Head

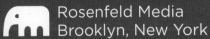

Rosenfeld Media
Brooklyn, New York

Designing Interface Animation
Meaningful Motion for User Experience
By Val Head

Rosenfeld Media, LLC

457 Third Street, #4R

Brooklyn, New York

11215 USA

On the Web: www.rosenfeldmedia.com

Please send errors to: errata@rosenfeldmedia.com

Publisher: Louis Rosenfeld

Managing Editor: Marta Justak

Interior Layout Tech: Danielle Foster

Cover Design: The Heads of State

Indexer: Sharon Shock

Proofreader: Sue Boshers

ISBN: 1-933820-32-2

ISBN-13: 978-1-933820-32-3

LCCN: 2016938558

Printed and bound in the United States of America

For Jason and Tucker

HOW TO USE THIS BOOK

Who Should Read This Book?

This book is for designers and developers who are interested in using animation in compelling ways in their work—on the web or in apps. This book doesn't cover how to code web animations; rather, it focuses on how to plan, prototype, and design them effectively. It will also help you convince your team, boss, or clients that animation is an important design tool worth using in your work.

Even if you don't design or develop interfaces directly, this book has some useful information for you as well. Team leads and product owners will find Chapters 9 through 11 especially helpful for uncovering ways that animation could improve their product and make animation part of their team's design process. Creative directors and art directors will find Chapter 9 useful for exploring the best ways to express the brands they work with in motion.

What's in This Book?

This book gives you the tools to design interface animations that help you create a better user experience and a higher level of style. It identifies the ways that animation can add to the experience and why these techniques work, while also giving you a primer in classic animation principles and motion design practices as applied to interface animation. You'll also learn modern principles of good interactive animation behavior. Combined, all this will help you create sophisticated and purposeful animation in your work.

Part I, "The Case for Animation," lays the groundwork, making the case for the potential benefits of animation in interfaces and how you can build on the craft of traditional animation in your own work. This section covers arguments you can make to advocate for the use of animation in your design work and breaks down how the classic principles of animation can be applied to interfaces. It also delves into recommendations for designing animations that behave well from the perspective of your users.

Chapter 1: Why You Can't Ignore Animation

Chapter 2: You Already Know More About Animation Than You Think

Chapter 3: Modern Principles of Interactive Animation

Part II, "Using Animation to Solve Design Principles," tackles the design problems that animation can help you solve, based on existing research and best practices in interface animation. Each chapter in this section covers a specific benefit of animation and how it can be used to its full potential, as well as multiple examples to demonstrate what works and why. You can apply the lessons learned from these examples to your own work.

Chapter 4: Using Animation to Orient and Give Context

Chapter 5: Using Animation to Direct Focus and Attention

Chapter 6: Using Animation to Show Cause and Effect

Chapter 7: Using Animation for Feedback

Chapter 8: Using Animation to Demonstrate

Chapter 9: Using Animation to Express Your Brand

Part III, "Animation in Your Work and Process," delves into how you can make animation a part of your design process. Realizing the power of animation as a design tool is one thing, but all that is lost if it's not something that is truly part of your process. The section explores different ways to consider animation at various points in your design process, as well as how to prototype and evaluate potential animations effectively. Last, but not least, it covers the practicalities of animating responsibly with your audience in mind.

Chapter 10: Where Animation Fits in Your Design Process

Chapter 11: Prototyping Your Animation Ideas

Chapter 12: Animating Responsibly

Conclusion: This Is Just the Beginning

What Comes with This Book?

This book's companion website (☎http://rosenfeldmedia.com/
books/designing-interface-animation/) contains a blog and
additional content. The book's diagrams and other illustrations are
available under a Creative Commons license (when possible) for you
to download and include in your own presentations. You can find
these on Flickr at www.flickr.com/photos/rosenfeldmedia/sets/.
The book's video examples are also available on Vimeo at
https://vimeo.com/album/3899826.

FREQUENTLY ASKED QUESTIONS

Is this book only about web animation?

I'm framing the majority of my discussion of animation around the web because that's my preferred medium; however, all of the theory and design approaches to using animation effectively apply to other platforms as well. Even if the technology of web animation isn't what you'll be working with, there are still many benefits you can gain from including animation in your design efforts.

Why talk about animation now?

The technology available on the web means that it's now possible to create effective animation using the same technologies that you've been using to build websites all along. At the same time, much of the audience's expectations have changed in recent years, due to the popularity of smartphones, touch screens, and similar devices. The combination of these two recent trends means that you should consider the potential design benefits of animation more closely. See page 4 for more information.

How can animation improve the user experience? How does it become more than just decoration or distraction?

Animation can improve feedback, aid in orientation, direct attention, show causality, and express your brand's personality. Great interface animation combines a known purpose and expert animation style to blend seamlessly into the rest of the design and enhance the experience. Identifying strong foundations of purpose for animation are covered in Chapters 4 through 9.

How do I convince my boss/client/team that animation is something we should use?

Getting your teammates or colleagues to view animation as a useful design tool takes time and won't happen overnight, but it can be done. The way to do this is to be an internal champion of animation and what it can add to your design efforts at every opportunity.

The more examples you can show to demonstrate what animation can offer design, the easier it will be for your colleagues to see the potential benefits of animation. See **page 164** for more advice on how to be an undercover animation hero.

How can I express my brand in motion?

Knowing your brand's personality and how it expresses itself in motion is key to creating a unique experience across many platforms and mediums. The same voice and tone your brand expresses with things like copy, content, type, and color can be expressed in animation terms as well. Depending on whether you are working with an established brand or a brand new venture, you may want to start with a motion audit—cataloging the animation that you already have—or by translating your brand's current personality traits to animation directly. See **Chapter 9** for more details on each approach and other tips for expressing your brand in motion.

Do Disney's classic principles of animation still apply to animating interfaces?

They absolutely do! While interface animation works in a different medium than these classic principles were originally written for, the concepts covered in the classic principles show you how to create animation that references the real world and communicates effectively—both of which are useful for designing effective interface animations. Much like you might reference the general guidelines of typography before delving into a layout with type, the classic principles can help guide your animation decisions. For more on the classic principles and how they apply to interface work, see **Chapter 2**.

How does animation affect the accessibility of an interface?

Animation can have both positive and negative effects on accessibility. It can help to make interfaces easier to understand by reducing cognitive load and making feedback or state changes easier to follow and understand. But it can also negatively affect people with vestibular disorders and similar conditions. For more on the potential impacts of animation on accessibility and how to animate responsibly, see Chapter 12.

CONTENTS

PART I: THE CASE FOR ANIMATION

CHAPTER 1

Why You Can't Ignore Animation   **3**

CHAPTER 2

You Already Know More About
Animation Than You Think   **15**

FOREWORD

Marc Davis, one of the original animators at Walt Disney Studios, once said that before the studio was formed, "Animation had been done before, but stories were never told."

I love that line. Not the least because it is some *powerful* shade being thrown at Disney's competitors, but because it was, in another sense, very true. At the time Disney founded his studio, animation was in a state of transition: it was evolving from an expensive, somewhat primitive and novel medium into a proper, respected, *moving* art form.

As you read these words, the web is undergoing a similar transition. And you've just opened a book that will guide you through it.

Early web animation was dominated by bold, evocative, and flashy work. But while there was wonderful work produced in the web's first days, *practical* web animation was a little harder to find. It's only in the last few years that web designers have come to appreciate what thoughtful, well-executed animation can do for them. When done right, a little motion can warm up an interface, to introduce a little playfulness to otherwise rote transactions. Animation can help us communicate more effectively with our audiences and make them feel more at home with our products, services, and designs.

This is the book Val Head has written for you: a foundational text for animation on the web. While practical tips abound throughout, she's not just concerned with the implementation. Not only will you learn *how* to build these designs, but also *why* certain techniques are more effective than others. In these pages, you'll learn from Val's vast library of interface examples and begin to develop your own animation vocabulary.

After all, animation on the web has been here for years. Now, it's time to tell stories—and Val's about to show you how.

—Ethan Marcotte,
author of *Responsive Web Design*

INTRODUCTION

I first encountered interfaced animation in a weekend workshop on Flash animation. I spent a few Saturdays learning the ins and outs of keyframes and ActionScript, and I was hooked. The fact that you could create animations that responded to input and make things move on-screen with code absolutely blew my mind at the time. It changed the way I thought of every interface I encountered from then on.

From there, I got into Flash and web design simultaneously. I loved the creativity and expressiveness that Flash allowed, and I also loved the openness and ubiquity of the web. For years, I was that weirdo designer who really liked both Flash and web standards and refused to take a side. At my first agency job, we would hold meetings to decide if a particular project was going to be built with web standards or Flash. Effectively, they were asking, "Are we going to make a boring static CSS site, or are we going to do something creative with this project?" It seemed like such a shame to let the technology determine how creative we could be with our work.

Thanks to the web animation technology of today, that is no longer a choice anyone has to make. You can make anything from a few tiny button transitions with CSS to a full-out 3D world with WebGL with web standards. Both those extremes, and anything along the way, can be achieved natively in your browser.

Why Now?

To borrow a phrase from the always eloquent web developer Jeremy Keith: we now have animation that is of the web, not just on the web. That's a big deal. Today's web animation can be built with the same tools we've always used to design and build the web: CSS and JavaScript. That is a huge amount of power and a vast arena in which to be creative. The possibilities this opens ups are enormous and exciting! It's truly a magical time to be designing for the web.

Animation on the web hasn't always felt magical, though. Even today, when web animation has already come so far from the obtuse and heavy Flash sites of the past, skip intros and banner ads are still the first thing many people think of when they hear the words *web* and *animation* in the same sentence.

Web animation is starting to come into its own, and every designer or developer who uses it in their work can influence what it will stand for in the future. You can have a hand in shaping what its new definition will be. I wrote this book to be a guide for how to embrace animation on the web as a positive, purposeful design tool. My hope is that it can help lay the groundwork for the new definition of what web animation will be. I'm very excited to see what it becomes.

The Case for Animation

The next three chapters in Part I, "The Case for Animation," will outline the reasons why you should consider animation in your UX design process, how looking to the past animation greats can make you better at designing animation, and how to plan animations that behave well in interactions. This is the information you can use to convince your boss or teammates (or maybe even yourself?) that animation is something worth using and looking into.

CHAPTER 1

Why You Can't Ignore Animation

The recent advancements in the animation field aren't the only reason there's a growing interest in web animation right now. A bigger reason is the fact that much of the audience has changed its attitude toward the screens.

Thanks to the popularity of smartphones and the blurring of lines between phones, tablets, and computers, the expectations of what interacting with an interface should feel like have changed. These small pocket-sized computers have become a part of daily life, and their interfaces feel more alive with their gestures, depth, and animation.

The increased use of interface animations started with smartphones and native apps, but now they can be found almost everywhere. Even major operating systems like Windows and OSX have begun using animation as a core part of their design and interactions.

In comparison, static interfaces—the kind that the web defaulted to for so long, due to a lack of options—can feel dated and even a bit dull. When compared, at best, they seem to lack the sophistication of interfaces that include animation as part of their design. At worst, static interfaces feel broken and frustrating. Well-designed animation is becoming part of the definition of sophisticated, current, and trustworthy design. Teams like the people behind Stripe Checkout have purposely used animation in their design efforts with the goal of designing a more sophisticated product.[1] It's a big reason why so many designers have started to look at animation more seriously. If your design goals include an interface that feels modern and sophisticated, well-designed animation is one of the ways to get there.

Recognizing that animation can make your designs feel modern and sophisticated is probably what got you curious about interface animation in the first place, too. The reasons why animation has that effect, and where animation can have the most positive impact, are a bit more nebulous. So let's look under the hood at the reasons why animation can make an interface feel more intuitive and easier to use.

---

1 Improve the Payment Experience with Animations: http://rfld.me/1qVnubI.

Animation Has Brain Benefits

Sometimes, you might feel that an animated solution you've come up with is easier to understand or follow than the non-animated version, but you can't put your finger on exactly why. Actually, your gut feeling is right, and it's more than just a feeling—there's research to back it up as well.

Once you start digging, you'll find a surprising number of academic studies have been done on the effectiveness of animation on different kinds of learning outcomes. One common theme that comes up in a number of research studies is that animating between the different states of your interface can reduce cognitive load for your users. Essentially, animating an element's movement makes that change in position visible on-screen, which means that your users don't have to keep track of where things have moved. The effort they would have used to track the object is essentially off-loaded from their brain to the visible animation on-screen. They expend less energy keeping track of where things are, and can then focus their efforts on more important things, such as your content or the task at hand. That's definitely a win-win situation.

TIP COGNITIVE LOAD DEFINED

Cognitive load refers to the total amount of mental effort being used in working memory.

A number of academic studies have researched different ways that animation can potentially reduce cognitive load. Among them, two studies from Erasmus University Rotterdam (2007) found that well-designed animation could reduce extraneous cognitive load for problem-solving tasks.[2] It also found that cueing techniques in complex animations could enhance learning performance and free up learners' working memory resources to focus on learning more efficiently.[3] A similar study from the University of New Mexico[4]

---

2 Making Instructional Animations More Effective: A Cognitive Load Approach, Paul Ayres and Fred Paas: http://rfld.me/1ScKuLV.

3 Attention Cueing as a Means to Enhance Learning from an Animation, B.B. de Koning (Björn), H.K. Tabbers (Huib), R.M.J.P. Rikers (Remy), and G.W.C. Paas (Fred) 2008-04-10: http://rfld.me/1S9UUtF.

4 Optimising Learning from Animations by Minimising Cognitive Load: Cognitive and Affective Consequences of Signalling and Segmentation Methods, Roxana Moreno: http://rfld.me/1YvF54j.

showed that students learning a specific skill with animated study aids outperformed other groups and reported lower levels of cognitive load.

The results of these studies, and others like them, can back up that gut feeling you get when an animated interface just feels easier to use. It feels easier because you, as the user, have to do less work to keep track of what's happening on-screen—a huge advantage of well-designed animation. Of course, the results of those studies don't mean that every interface out there can be improved with animation alone. But they do prove that there is a strong potential for animation to be beneficial in the right context. (See Chapters 4-8.)

Reducing cognitive load is a big plus, but the potential brain benefits of animation don't stop there. Other studies have shown that animation can improve decision-making capabilities[5] and even help people learn and remember spatial relationships.[6] Helping users keep track of spatial relationships is a big plus. Spatial relationships in an interface become more and more important as you find yourself designing for different-sized screens. The limited screen real estate on smaller screens means that it's just not possible to have every available interface item on-screen at all times. Animation can help make it clear which items have moved off-screen and where they can be found again.

Establishing spatial relationships with animation can be equally helpful for interfaces that have different content on different layers as well. It doesn't have to be limited to objects that are out of view to the left and right of the screen. It can also be more temporal and related to which layer in a stack of layers you're currently viewing. Transitioning between the layers can help demonstrate what order the layers of the interface are stacked in and how your users can navigate between them.

That's the highlight reel of academic research on animation as it applies to interface design. If you find these facts interesting, you can follow the nearly endless trail of research papers by looking at each study's references list. Not all of the references apply as directly to interface animation as the ones mentioned here, but they all reveal some interesting facts about human behavior and computers.

---

5 Does Animation in User Interfaces Improve Decision Making? Cleotilde Gonzalez: **http://rfld.me/1Qa1VbH**.

6 Does Animation Help Users Build Mental Maps of Spatial Information? Benjamin B. Bederson, and Angela Boltman: **http://rfld.me/23IkGwh**.

Animation and *motion* are two terms that tend to be used interchangeably, especially when discussing interface animation. Most of the time, there's nothing wrong with that, but sometimes for the sake of clarity, it's important to highlight the differences between the two terms.

Animation is defined as changing some property over time. On the other hand, *motion* is the act of moving or the process of being moved. Their meanings are very similar, but there is one key difference: an object that is animated doesn't necessarily have to move. For example, you can animate nonmotion properties of an object like opacity, or blur. The appearance of the object will change over the course of the animation, but there won't be any movement involved. That is definitely animation, but it's not motion.

To put it more simply, *all motion is animation, but not all animation is motion.* Their meanings overlap a lot, but they aren't exactly the same.

Animation Communicates

Animation adds yet another dimension to your design work—the dimension of time—and it communicates on a different level than your other design tools, such as type or color. It's human nature to assign meaning to why something is moving, based on your experience with real-world physics or by anthropomorphizing the animated objects.

When you see something move on-screen, you look for a reason as to why it moved the way it did. Did another object push it? Is it falling? Did it bounce off the edge of the screen or another object? All of those questions (and others like them) are ways you might try to explain motion on-screen based on your experience with real-world physics. After all, you've spent a lot of time in the real world, and you're very familiar with how it works. By looking for an explanation of the motion in the realm of what you already know, you can make what you're seeing on-screen feel more familiar.

Physical things like gravity and friction don't actually apply to animation on a screen, but you still evaluate the movement you see on-screen based on what you know of the real world.[7] This is why

---

7 Animating Anthropomorphism: Giving Minds to Geometric Shapes, Jason G. Goldman on March 8, 2013: **http://rfld.me/1SiOaRa** or **https://archive.is/aojec**.

interface animation that reflects some aspects of the physical world feels more familiar. And conversely, it's why interface animation that significantly contrasts with what you see in the physical world without good reason can be so disorienting or unsettling.

Sometimes, the objects on-screen can even seem like they have personalities, motivations, or emotions—essentially anthropomorphizing these objects into characters. A 1944 Smith College study by Fritz Heider and Marianne Simmel[8] found that the vast majority of participants who were shown a film of animated geometric shapes interpreted the shapes as characters and created a story to explain the shapes' movements. The shapes were triangles, lines, and other simple shapes—and there was no actual story at play. Still, nearly all of the participants saw one. Your users will find similar emotional ties and motivations in the animations you design, regardless of whether or not you put it there intentionally.

Knowing that your animations will be interpreted through one or both of those lenses—applying the rules of the physical world or as characters—creates a solid case for consciously designing what you want your animations to say. No matter what you do, they will be saying something. You can leave this additional message up to chance, or you can intentionally design it, taking advantage of that additional layer of communication to connect with your audience. It seems like a waste to pass up a chance to communicate something meaningful.

Animation Connects Contexts

Animation is a valuable design tool for creating a common feel throughout your design, even when it's viewed in different contexts or on different devices. Designing an experience that feels cohesive and connected, despite the fact that your audience might be using any device under the sun to access your work, and maybe even more than one of them at once, is a big challenge of modern web design. Even in the world of native apps, your users are likely to encounter your product's mobile app, desktop app, and website all within a short window of time. The considered use of animation can help you tie the experience together by creating a common feel across all those contexts.

---

8 The film from the Fritz Heider and Marianne Simmel study: http://rfld.me/1MwhYpu.

The current responsive web design (RWD) landscape makes it especially important to unify the experience in some way across all the various contexts and devices your audience may be viewing your work on. You can use animation as a way to connect these contexts and create a common feel across all mediums and contexts. In fact, it's a very powerful one. Considering the big picture of how all your interface animations appear as a group is a big part of doing animation well.

Even if RWD isn't a specific concern for you, your audience will encounter your product or brand in a variety of ways—on their phones, laptops, in ads, on social media, and more—and the more common threads of design you have that can make all these contexts feel related or connected, the better. Even when you're dealing with apps authored for different platforms from a different codebase, intentionally designing common threads in how your animation looks and behaves can help make them feel more consistent. When you have interface elements that animate in a similar manner on screens of all sizes or platforms, that's one more thing that can remain constant, even while things like the layout may change.

The way all the individual interface animations you design work together at the big-picture level is what affects how connected these different contexts can be. By considering the choreography for all your animations as a group, you can better control the common factors that are communicated with animation across different layouts and viewport sizes. Two ways that the design of your animations as a whole can bridge the gaps between contexts are:

- Considering the choreography of the UI
- Giving similar content items similar animation behaviors

UI Choreography

Having a considered plan for the choreography of your interface animations can also help tie the experiences together and make them feel like one cohesive entity. Traditional choreographers design sequences for dances or shows, making sure that all the dance steps and movements work together as a whole. Considering UI choreography is a bit like playing director or choreographer with all the interface animations you design. As you plan the actions and movements of the elements on-screen (your "actors"), you're also checking back with the big picture view to make sure that the overall message is intact and that all the actors are working as a cohesive ensemble.

When your animation's personality doesn't match the personality of your brand, things can feel off. For years, Apple's navigation on **apple.com** was completely mismatched to its brand (see Figure 1.1). This animation drove me a little crazy every time I saw it, and I was surprised it was left unchanged for years. (Thankfully, it was redesigned in 2015 right around the release of the iPhone 6s, but it had been on Apple's site since at least 2011.)

The animation was exaggerated as each product scaled bouncily into place and then zipped off out of sight, making an equally bouncy exit. The products moved in and out more like happy dancing Muppets than the sleek streamlined products they really were. The animation didn't match the personality of the product, or the brand for that matter. That made it stand out for the wrong reasons.

FIGURE 1.1

Apple.com's old menu animations didn't fit the simple sleek nature of its brand. You can see the old menu in action in this video: **https://vimeo.com/162711355.**

That mismatched motion didn't stop anyone from buying their next Apple product, and it didn't render the whole design a failure. But it was a missed opportunity to use a consistent voice across all aspects of the design. I'm sure I wasn't the only one who paused to wonder why it was bouncing around like that.

Compare the feeling of mismatched design and animation to the UI animation in the game *Dots*. The transitions applied to the menus and settings screens echo the motion found in the game.

The animation, even while you're just editing settings, fits the mood of the app and reinforces its brand by using transitions that echo the ones you see during game play (see Figure 1.2). Pretty clever, right? You can almost picture a conductor conducting each bit of motion to ensure that each fits into the bigger picture. In fact, it fits so well, you may have hardly given it a second thought until someone pointed it out.

FIGURE 1.2
The *Dots'* game setting menu from around the same time had the same kind of animation, but it fit the personality of its brand and game. You can see it in action in this video: **https://vimeo.com /162712539**.

A key part of designing good UI animations is remembering that adding animation is an opportunity to communicate a little something more. Any motion you add is going to communicate something; it's really more a question of whether it's saying what you'd like it to say.

A cohesive-feeling UI choreography can be achieved by designing all your interface animations to have similar or shared traits. The more they seem to match, the more they'll feel as if they're working together.

On a more granular level, you can use animation to reinforce commonalities among similar content items. Animation can be used as an additional clue to help inform the purpose or nature of different kinds of content. You likely do this already with things like color and typography. For example, all your navigation items probably have a similar look and feel to them with the colors and shapes they use. Using similar animation for all of them will strength this connection.

You can use animation to reinforce hierarchy within these groups of similar content as well. For example, you might have all the buttons on a site use the same blue-to-green color change animation, except for the delete button, which has a blue-to-red color fade. That would establish a common behavior for all buttons—they change color when activated. But the delete button has a slight variation on that behavior to help make the importance and severity of clicking it more apparent.

TIP **DON'T FORGET THE VIDEOS**

Many of the figures in this book have corresponding videos to show you their animation in action. Don't forget to watch these videos to get the full picture!

Animation Grabs Attention

Of all the design tools at your disposal when designing for the web, animation is the one most likely to use its outside voice. Motion gets people's attention,[9] especially motion in the periphery of their vision. That's the motivation behind animated banner ads vying for your attention while you try to read an article online. It's even the driving force behind those silly windsock creatures outside car dealerships that try to catch your eye as you drive down the highway. In general, it's hard for you *not* to look when you see something moving out of the corner of your eye. In the past, that instinct was probably used to

---

9 It's Alive! Animate Motion Captures Visual Attention, Pratt, J., Radulescu, P., Guo, R.M., and Abrams, R.A. (2010). *Psychological Science*, 21, 1724–1730: http://rfld.me/1WuaaXp.

save humankind from terrible danger, but now it's mostly just used to exploit and annoy you.

The attention-grabbing powers of animation can be used in more positive ways. Using it well, and with more positive intentions, gives you the ability to reinforce the hierarchy of content and to highlight what's most important at a specific point in time. Color, type, and layout can be used to create a static hierarchy, and animation can add to that by reacting to actions or timing that changes what is most important at any given time. In Chapter 5, "Using Animation to Direct Focus and Attention," we'll cover some specific tactics you can use to direct attention with animation, based on what's most important to your users.

Animation's potential to communicate, connect, get attention, and reduce things like cognitive load lays the groundwork for what animation can offer to interface design. By basing your use of animation on these known strengths and researched benefits, you can use animation more effectively in your work and support your decision to use it better. Grounding your reasons for using animation in one or more of these high-level areas can be a very effective way to sell the idea of interface animation to your boss or colleagues. In the following chapters, we'll dig into the details of exactly how to harness these potential benefits of animation in your own work and how to do it all with an expert sense of style.

Staying on Point

The high-level benefits of designing interfaces with animation in mind are:

- It has potential brain benefits, like reducing cognitive load, reducing change blindness, and better communicating spatial relationships.

- It communicates on a different level than things like type and color.

- Animation can be a constant in the experiences you design across devices, screen sizes, and platforms.

- Animation's ability to grab attention can be used to reinforce content hierarchy.

- It can be used to reinforce your brand's personality and values.

CHAPTER 2

You Already Know More About Animation Than You Think

As a kid, Saturday mornings were the best part of my weekend. My sister and I would grab our comfy spots on the couch and settle in to watch our favorite cartoons. It's funny to think that while spending that time plopped in front of the TV, I was also absorbing some of the key principles of animation. I just didn't know it yet.

The classic principles of animation are the foundation of most motion graphics and animation work. They make a great foundation for interface animation work as well. If you've spent any time watching animated feature films or cartoons, you've likely encountered these principles in action many times already, too.

It's not often you read an article or post about animation that doesn't reference the classic principles of animation at least in passing. Sometimes, they're referred to as just *The Principles of Animation* or the *12 Basic Principles of Animation* or some similar variation. The classic principles all of those article are referring to are the ones found in Disney's *Illusion of Life* book (see Figure 2.1).[1] Authored by two Disney animators, Ollie Johnston and Frank Thomas, and first published in the early 1980s, the book was Disney's way of revealing its secrets of great life-like animation to the world. Ever since then, it has been regarded as a bible of animation.

The 12 classic principles only make up a single chapter in this book, but they are indispensable for creating animation with a lifelike, relatable feel. As you read about each in more detail, they'll almost certainly sound familiar, and you'll likely even be able to picture each in your head using your favorite animated characters.

The 12 classic principles according to *The Illusion of Life* are the following:

- Timing
- Follow-through and overlapping action
- Anticipation
- Secondary action
- Arcs
- Squash and Stretch
- Slow In and Slow Out

---

1 *The Illusion of Life: Disney Animation*: http://rfld.me/1V4mrT8.

- Exaggeration

- Straight Ahead and Pose to Pose

- Solid Drawing

- Appeal

- Staging

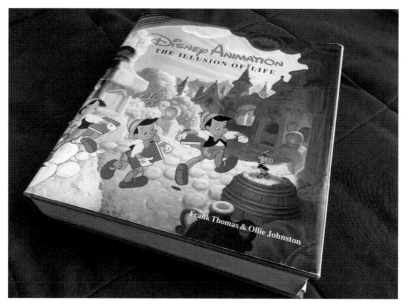

FIGURE 2.1
My well-worn copy of *The Illusion of Life*.

Not Just for Cartoons

Working in the digital space, it's unlikely that your primary job is to animate cartoon characters. But even when working with different subjects—images, text, and interface elements—making your design choices based on the 12 principles will improve the way the animation you design looks and feels. The 12 principles describe how to create lifelike movements in a medium that is not actually real life, which is very useful for interfaces. Lifelike animation feels more natural and connects better with audiences. Animations that reference the real world and how objects behave make for a more satisfying and emotionally connected experience.

Besides better-looking animation, studying the 12 principles will also give you a more robust vocabulary for describing animation. Learning these concepts and their definitions means that you and your team can specifically discuss detailed aspects of the motion you're designing using terms with common meanings for everyone. It's much easier to implement feedback like "That animation needs more oomph, so let's give it more follow-through" than just "That animation needs more oomph."

I cover the 12 principles in this chapter based on which ones I think have the biggest impact on interface animation. It's still worth being familiar with the ones that don't apply as directly to your work right now, too, but I've covered them last as they aren't always as applicable. Also, don't feel like you have to memorize every single principle and its definition right away. You can always check back to this chapter or Google the definition of each while you're working later.

Timing (and Spacing) Really Are Everything

Timing and spacing go hand in hand to describe the foundational principle of animation. Together these principles create the illusion of an animated object obeying the laws of physics. The speed at which an object moves and how it changes speed during that motion tells you a lot about both the object in motion and the forces that might be acting upon it. For example, the way a bowling ball bounces is very different from how a ping-pong ball bounces—that's timing and spacing in action.

NOTE TIMING VS. SPACING

Note that *The Illusion of Life* refers to both these concepts only as *timing*. Later animation texts split up the concept into timing and spacing, which has become the more common convention today.

Timing and spacing convey the mood, emotion, and reaction of an object. The latter is especially important for interface animations. The laws of physics don't apply on-screen, so there's no obligation to imitate them precisely, but your audience will always be trying to determine why it is the objects you animate move or change the way they do. Users subconsciously pick up on cues about an object's personality or the forces that might be acting on it, just by seeing it animate. Paying close attention to timing and spacing puts you in control of what your animations are saying, instead of leaving it up to chance.

In *Timing for Animation* (yes, an entire book devoted entirely to timing and spacing) John Halas and Harold Whitaker sum up the importance of timing perfectly: "Timing is the part of animation which gives meaning to movement. Movement can easily be achieved by drawing the same thing in two different positions and inserting a number of other drawings between the two. The result on the screen will be movement but it will not be animation."[2]

Timing

Timing is the amount of time it takes for an action to happen, the duration of a particular movement or change. Envisioning timing is easiest using the classic example of a bouncing ball. Each bounce of the ball is an action, and the duration of each bounce conveys something about the forces acting on the ball. The timing of the ball bouncing across the floor is marked with diamond shapes in Figure 2.2.

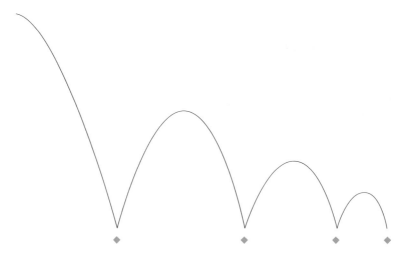

FIGURE 2.2
Each bounce of the ball is an action, and the diamonds here represent the timing of each action.

2 Harold Whitaker and John Halas, *Timing for Animation*: http://www.focalpress.com/books/details/9780240521602/.

The timing of each bounce in this bouncing ball animation conveys information about the ball itself, based on what you know of the physical world. The duration of each bounce of the ball gives you some clues about the forces acting on the ball. Each bounce gets shorter as forces like gravity overtake the momentum of the ball's movement, and the number of bounces suggests this might be a fairly light ball, or one that was dropped with a lot of force.

In the digital world, timing is generally the duration of an animation. In many cases, depending on the technology you use, you'll likely be setting the duration explicitly in code. In interface animation, good timing is the difference between a transition that happens seamlessly within the experience and one that makes you wait excessively for it to finish before you can move on. That goes a bit beyond just the speed of an action, but we'll dig into that more in Chapter 3, "Modern Principles of Interactive Animation."

Spacing

Spacing, quite literally, fills in the gaps of timing. Spacing is the changes in speed over the duration of an action's timing. How long an action takes place tells you a lot about the object involved in that action, but its changes in speed over the course of that action tell even more.

Spacing gets its name from the way speed changes are created with frame-by-frame animation. At a constant frame rate, two frames that are drawn closer together show that change happening more slowly. Two frames drawn farther apart show that change happening more quickly when played back. In the digital world, spacing is most often expressed by the easing or timing functions you use. You won't be drawing individual frames yourself, but the browser or other rendering methods will be doing that for you under the hood.

Taking that same bouncing ball example with a snapshot of each frame exposed, you can see the spacing and how it affects the changes in speed over each bouncing action (see Figure 2.3). When the ball is falling downward and picking up speed, the frames are spaced farther apart. Near the top of each bounce, the ball is moving slower, battling the forces of gravity to get just a little higher, and thus the frames are spaced closer together. Over that same amount of time a frame takes up, the ball has made a smaller change in position than when it was falling downward.

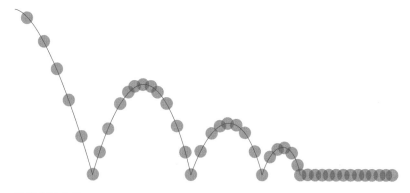

FIGURE 2.3

The spacing of the individual frames of the ball bounce changes the speed of the ball at the various stages of its bounce.

For web animation, spacing comes down to the easing (also called the *timing function* in CSS) applied to an animating property.[3] Easing determines how speed changes occur across the duration of an animation. That easing is the biggest indicator of the mood and personality of the object.

The spacing (or easing) of an animation can say a lot about the physical traits of an object in motion or the forces acting upon it. On the most basic level, spacing can make an object appear to be obeying the laws of physics as we know them. Take these two squares, animated to move from left to right across the screen, in this demo shown in Figure 2.4, for example.[4] The top square has been assigned "ease-in-out" for its easing, which means it will speed up into its movement, move fastest in the middle of its movement, and then slow down to reach its target position. The square on the bottom has been assigned "linear" for its easing, which means it will move at a constant speed across the entire movement from start to finish with no changes in speed. It starts abruptly and ends abruptly.

In the demo, the top square's motion looks more natural. It moves in a way that a real-life object might, accelerating into its motion and slowing to a stop. The way it speeds up and slows down gives the suggestion of it having weight as well. The bottom square, with its linear

---

3 Timing function for CSS: https://drafts.csswg.org/css-transitions /#transition-timing-function-property.

4 Ease-in-out vs. linear easing example: http://rfld.me/23F4Qmb.

easing, looks more mechanical and offers little information about the object itself. The only thing different between the two is the easing they use, and it makes a big difference even with this simple motion.

FIGURE 2.4

The top circles represent an ease-in-out style of easing, while the bottom circles show linear easing. Like the animated squares in the live example (**http://rfld.me/23F4Qmb**), the speed changes of ease-in-out style easing are closer to natural movement.

Timing and spacing are just as important now as they were back in the early days of animation. While they may be expressed differently—mostly with duration and easing instead of frame-by-frame drawings—they are still the foundation on which many of the other principles are based, as well as the foundation of good animation. Paying attention to the timing and spacing of your animations will accelerate your animation skills exponentially. The mark of a good animator is a good sense of timing. That takes time to develop (no pun intended), but the more you animate, the better your sense of timing will become.

TIP TIMING AND SPACING AS EXPLAINED BY TED

This TED-Ed video is one of my favorite explanations of timing and spacing. It explains everything you need to know about these two concepts in under seven minutes: **https://www.youtube.com/watch?v=KRVhtMxQWRs**.

Easing Curves Explained

Many coding languages and animation tools have some built-in defaults for easing, such as *ease-in, ease-out, ease-in-out,* and *linear.* The keywords in CSS are all based on Cubic-Bézier functions, and you can also create your own custom curves, giving you nearly infinite easing choices with animation. Custom motion curves are what allow you to be more expressive with your spacing choices.

Cubic-Bézier functions can be expressed as a function with four numbers or visualized as a curve. The numbers are what shows up in your code, but they are more difficult to read at a glance. For example, Cubic-Bézier (0.42,0,0.58,1) doesn't hold a whole lot of meaning unless you've put in some time memorizing Cubic-Bézier values (which is not a thing most people have any interest in doing). Looking at the curve that same Cubic-Bézier function represents, however, is much easier to interpret at a glance.

Here's how the function and the curve are related: the four numbers in the Cubic-Bézier function represent two x and y coordinates—think of it as Cubic-Bézier (x1,y1,x2,y2), which can be plotted on a graph. Those two x,y coordinates represent the position of the Bézier control handles, which work a lot like the small handles you move around in Adobe Illustrator with the pen tool (see Figure 2.5).

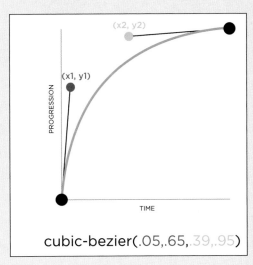

FIGURE 2.5
The position of the Bézier handles defines the shape of the easing curve much like working with the pen tool in Illustrator or similar vector tools.

sidebar continues on next page

Cubic-Bézier motion graphs plot the progression of an animation against the time it takes for that animation to complete. The start and end points are fixed, and the shape of the curve is influenced by two Bézier handles. The position of those two handles are what the two x and y coordinates in the Cubic-Bézier function describe.

The flatter parts of the curve indicate a slower rate of change in the animation, and the steeper parts of the curve indicate a faster rate of change in the animating property. Based on that, the curve above indicates an animation that starts quickly and slows down as it reaches the end of the animation. That also means it's a variation of ease-out style easing. With custom Cubic-Bézier curves, you can fine-tune exactly how much it eases out and control precisely when and how fast those speed changes occur. To try that out for yourself, view this same curve on **cubic-bezier.com (http://cubic-bezier.com/#.05,.65,.39,.95)**, where you can manipulate the points in real time to adjust the curve and then preview the motion in your browser. There is a lot of power in those curves!

You can find Cubic-Bézier editors and custom Cubic-Bézier curves in places other than **cubic-bezier.com**, too. Some code editors and prototyping software, like Atom or Principle, for example, have editing tools built into them, so you can create custom curves easily while working. There are also some Sass libraries that come with a list of predefined Cubic-Bézier functions, based on the popular Penner Easing Equations. Both the Firefox and Chrome browsers have Cubic-Bézier editors built into their developer tools as well. All of these options can save you time finding and customizing motion curves.

Follow-Through and Overlapping Action

Classically, follow-through refers to the fact that not everything in motion comes to a stop at once. Imagine a bulldog with big droopy jowls. When he turns his head to the right, his droopy jowls would keep moving just a little farther to the right, even after his head stopped turning, and then they would settle back in to place. That's follow-through in a nutshell.

In interfaces, follow-through manifests in a slightly different way. It's often shown by having an object overshoot its target position and then settle into its final position (see Figure 2.6). Follow-through can make it seem as if the object had so much energy and momentum that it just couldn't stop in time. Follow-through can be paired with skewing the object slightly as well, to make it look like the top of the object just couldn't come to a stop as quickly as the bottom half of the object did.

FIGURE 2.6

This modal in the *Two Dots* game creates follow-through by overshooting its destination, overshooting just slightly off-screen. The counting up animation also starts before the entrance animation completes, creating some overlapping action as well. You can see it in action in this video: **https://vimeo.com/162712104**.

Achieving Follow-Through in Code

There are a couple of ways you can achieve follow-through with CSS or JavaScript-based animations. The simplest way is to select an easing option that causes the object in motion to overshoot its destination and then settle back in place (see Figure 2.7). A Cubic-Bézier function that extends out of its bounding box just before the end of the animation will do the trick here. You just need to set the starting and ending position for the motion, and the easing curve will take care of creating the follow-through for you.

Easing curves derived from different mathematical sources that have a similar shape will also work. Adjusting the exact shape of the curve will change the amount of follow-through you'll get and how amplified the overshoot is.

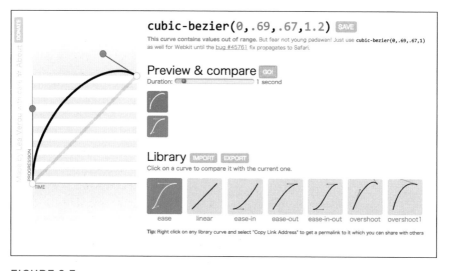

FIGURE 2.7

This Cubic-Bézier curve will result in follow-through because the curve extends out of the graph boundaries beyond the end state of the animation.

For more fine-grained control of the follow-through, or to create more complex follow-through action, you'll want to add additional keyframes to the animation beyond the starting and ending position. With CSS, that would mean changing your @keyframes rule to read something like this pseudo code:

```
@keyframes overshoot {
    0% - be at the starting position
    95% - move to a position just a little bit past the end position
    100% - go to the end position and stop
}
```

Adding keyframes to the animation, in whatever language or tool you choose, gives you added control over the follow-through action, since you can manually adjust the easing used between each keyframe and explicitly spell out the change in position you want to see with the additional keyframe values. This approach will make it easier to add to the action by animating some child elements as well. You can see both approaches to creating follow-through with CSS in this demo: http://rfld.me/1RUg7Lm.

Overlapping Action and Offsets

Overlapping action is closely related to follow-through—it represents the concept that a character doesn't wait for one action to be completely finished before starting the next. For example, the bulldog turning his head to look at a tasty bone would start reaching for the bone before the action of his head turn (and the follow-through of his jowls) was finished.

In interfaces, you can use overlapping action for related animation in a similar way. When you're animating a series of animations that happen in order, you don't have to wait for the first one to finish completely before starting the second. Often, this behavior is called *offsets*, which is a version of overlapping action.

You may hear about animating with offsets in discussions of motion graphics or title design because it's usually applied to objects instead of characters. Some JavaScript animation libraries have staggers, which are essentially the same concept as offsets. Offsets come into play when you're animating a group of similar objects in order, a group of list items, for example. Instead of having them enter all at once as a group, each list item starts its entrance a little after the one before it, offsetting the animations by a fraction of a second. With CSS and JavaScript, this effect is most often achieved by delaying each subsequent animation by just a little more than the one before it, essentially staggering the delays of the animations, as shown in this CSS-based demo: http://rfld.me/1NopUnl. Offsets create a subtle wave-like motion that is much more pleasing to the eye, while also reinforcing the independence of each item within the group (see Figure 2.8).

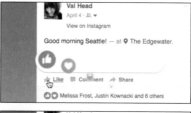

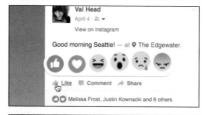

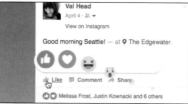

FIGURE 2.8
Facebook's Reactions icons appear using offset motion as each emoticon's entrance starts its entrance a fraction of a second after the one before it, creating a staggered wave-like pattern. You can see it in action in this video: **https://vimeo.com/162712106.**

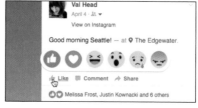

Anticipation

Anticipation is the inverse of follow-through, and the two are often used together to create an increased sense of energy. Anticipation is a small movement in preparation for the larger action that is about to take place. Take, for example, the golfer's backswing before she hits the ball, or the baseball pitcher's windup before tossing a fastball.

Very few movements in real life occur without some kind of anticipation hinting at what is about to happen next. That's why using this principle in interfaces can help make movements seem more lifelike or relatable to your audience.

Like follow-through, anticipation in interface animation tends to be a bit more subdued than in real life. For example, an object on-screen may move or lean slightly in the opposite direction before zipping off-screen—almost like it is charging up its energy before making the move (see Figure 2.9). The larger this anticipatory movement, the more energy, or even playfulness, the moving object appears to have.

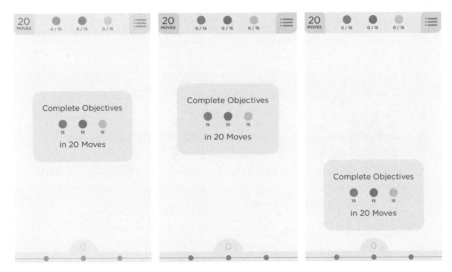

FIGURE 2.9
The *Dots* game uses anticipation in its modal dialogue's exit animations. The modal moves upward just slightly in anticipation of making its exit down out the bottom of the screen. You can see these in action, along with a variation of this motion that **Soundcloud.com** uses in this video: **https://vimeo.com/162712110**.

Achieving Anticipation in Code

To create anticipation with CSS or JavaScript, you have much the same options as you do with follow-through but in reverse. To achieve it with your easing choice, you could select a Cubic-Bézier function that dips outside of the graph bounds at the beginning of the curve (see Figure 2.10).

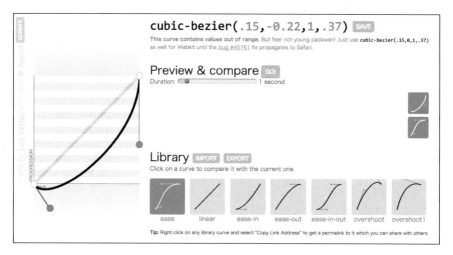

FIGURE 2.10

A Cubic-Bézier curve that will result in anticipation because the curve extends out of the graph bounds beyond the beginning position of the animation.

For more precision or to create a more complex effect, you can add additional keyframes at the beginning of your animation to create that small movement in the opposite direction at the start of the action. The keyframes would look like something similar to this pseudo code if you were animating an object moving from left to right:

```
@keyframes anticipate {
    0% - the starting position
    5% - move to a position just a bit to the left
    100% - move to the end position to the far right of the screen
}
```

You can see both approaches to creating follow-through with CSS in this demo: http://rfld.me/22uxCU1.

Secondary Action

Secondary action is defined as any additional motion that complements, or supports, the primary motion. Secondary action is like the supporting actor of animation. In traditional animation, this might be something like a character whistling or moving her arms around while she walks. Those additional actions inform the walking movement, showing that she's happy in this case. In interfaces, it's how elements in close proximity move in reaction to the main motion.

Opportunities for secondary action interfaces aren't always as obvious as they might be with characters. However, many interface elements do have related elements, child elements, and elements that move together. Those are prime candidates for secondary action.

Sometimes, the pieces creating the secondary action are only temporarily there to heighten the primary motion. One example of secondary action that you may have seen quite often is Twitter's "like heart" animation. The main action in that animation is the heart scaling up and then back into place as a pink heart representing a liked Tweet (see Figure 2.11). The additional circles and particles that help make it seem more like the heart is bursting out into view are the secondary action.

Secondary action that's illustrative like the Twitter heart animation is often accomplished with sprite animations. A long (or tall) image with each stage of the animation drawn into it is animated as a background image, like a film strip to create the animation. You can see the Twitter heart animation in action here: **https://vimeo .com/162712112**. For interface elements with child elements, you can also create secondary action by applying complementary motion to the child elements when the parent element moves.

FIGURE 2.11
The full sprite image of Twitter's "like heart" animation. The circles and particles that animate around the heart in Twitter's "like heart" animation are examples of secondary action.

Arcs

The principle of arcs is one of the few that is actually harder to pull off in the digital world than the hand-drawn animation world. Computers are very good at creating precise motion in straight lines. Nearly everything in real life, on the other hand, doesn't move in precise straight lines at all. Most movements in real life follow a slightly curved path as opposed to a straight line, and that is the concept of arcs. Imagine yourself raising your arm to point at something in front of you. Even though it might feel like you've moved your arm in a completely straight line, you probably haven't, at least not if you're moving naturally.

Working in digital, most of your tools work off x and y coordinates. Since the shortest distance between two points is a straight line, most tools will create motion paths that are straight lines by default. Digging a little deeper and purposely moving objects along a slightly curved, or arced, path conveys a sense of more natural motion.

An example of arcs in interface animation is Safari's file download animation, as shown in Figure 2.12. When you select a file to download from Safari, an icon animates out of the browser window to your downloads folder, following a curved path.

FIGURE 2.12
Safari's save file animation follows an arced path from the download link to the downloads folder in your dock. I've superimposed the approximate arc followed in this image, and you can see it in action in this video: **https://vimeo.com/162712118.**

Achieving Arcs in Code

To achieve arcs in web animation, you need to turn to motion paths and assign a curved path for your animation to follow. Currently, this can be done with SMIL (synchronized multimedia integration language) in SVG (http://rfld.me/1NaQRAu), although that's being deprecated, and also with the Greensock (https://greensock.com/) animation library. In the near future, CSS will also be getting the ability to create motion along a path (https://www.w3.org/TR/motion-1/), which will make arcs even easier to pull off on the web.

Squash and Stretch

Squash and stretch is the concept that when real-life objects are in motion—especially parts of living beings—they deform slightly, based on that motion. The classic example is the bouncing ball. It will deform, or squash, when it hits the ground and stretch back out to its true shape as it bounces upward from there.

The amount of squash observed indicates what kind of material the ball might be made out of. How ridged it is or how soft it is will be apparent by how much it squashes when it hits the ground. If it were an especially soft ball, it might even stretch as it's falling at its highest speed. It might not occur noticeably in real life, but stretching it while it was moving fastest would help emphasize how quickly it's moving (see Figure 2.13).

FIGURE 2.13

This dripping menu on **animalmade.com** shows squash and stretch in action. Each drop stretches as it accelerates downward. You can see it in action in this video: **https://vimeo.com/162712115**.

Achieving Squash and Stretch in Code

Getting some squash and stretch in your CSS or JavaScript-based animations can be as simple as adding a scale transform on the same axis that an object is moving. For example, if you were moving an object from left to right, you could scale it to 120% on the x axis as it hit its top speed. That would show it stretching as it was moving at its fastest speed. Then it would squash back to its normal width on the x axis, or maybe even a bit farther as it slowed down, depending on the effect you wanted to create. You can see that simple squash and stretch in action in this demo: http://rfld.me/1WrZV6a.

Squash and stretch can get a lot more complex than that, of course. The more complex transforms required to create a more detailed squash and stretch animation can be handled well by the matrix transform and matrix3d transform properties of CSS. Those properties can be daunting to attempt to write yourself, so thankfully there are tools like BounceJS (http://bouncejs.com) that provide a visual editor for complex transforms and export animation code that you can copy and paste into your own project to reuse the effect.

In *The Illusion of Life*, Thomas and Johnston stated that squash and stretch was the most important principle for realistic character animation. It's less important when animating interfaces instead of characters, but employing this principle even in small amounts injects a large amount of lifelike feeling to your work. Squash and stretch is one of the hardest principles to master and also an easy one to overdo. A well-designed squash and stretch effect maintains the same physical volume for the object, no matter how far it's squashed or stretched. Too much squash and stretch can read as childish or sloppy. It's an effect that takes a lot of practice and iteration to get just right. Don't let that stop you from trying it, though. When done well, it adds great energy and life to your animations.

Slow In and Slow Out

Slow in and slow out refers to the spacing of frames across an animated action. Objects that move at a uniform speed across an entire action seem mechanical and lacking life. (Just like we saw with linear easing earlier in this chapter.) Real-world objects tend to gain speed as they start moving, move fastest in the middle of their movement, and then slow down before coming to a stop. So there is a slowing of velocity, or more closely spaced frames drawn, and the beginning and end of each movement, which, when drawn frame by frame, looks something like Figure 2.14.

FIGURE 2.14

The principle of slow in and slow out is achieved easily by using some variation of ease-in-out easing.

That figure should look familiar, too. You looked at it earlier in this chapter when discussing spacing. Slow in and slow out describes a specific variation of spacing that best reflects how things move organically in real life. You can see it in action in CSS in this demo: http://rfld.me/1NopVYx.

Achieving Slow In and Slow Out in Code

With digital tools, slow in and slow out equates to variations of ease-in-out easing (meaning, not necessarily the ease-in-out CSS keyword, but any easing curve that has a similar shape to it), and it's often there by default. With CSS, if you don't select a timing function (easing) for an animation or transition, it will be assigned "ease" by default. And this default is a variation of slow in and slow out. Of course, that may not be the slow in and slow out that you want for your animation, but it's an option for you.

Most JavaScript libraries have a number of variations of ease-in-out easing that meet the criteria for slow in and slow out as well. Easing presets like "easeInOutQuad," "easeInOutSine," and similar ones will all be some variation of slow in and slow out. Custom easing curves are always an option as well. When working in the digital space, you may never have to create slow in and slow out manually, but it's important to be aware of when and how your tools are making these decisions for you.

Slow in and slow out doesn't mean having to use the same ease-in-out easing for everything. The rate at which an object gains speed as it starts moving and the rate at which it slows as it stops can vary greatly and still fit the principle of slow in and slow out. Also, you don't always see the full motion of objects that move into view from off-screen, or move out of view and finish their animation off-screen. So don't feel that this principle means that every single animation must have an ease-in-out easing applied to it.

Exaggeration

Exaggeration means making the core action or meaning of an animation more apparent and real. The principle was a result of Walt Disney telling his animators to make the action more convincing. A character winding his arm up dramatically before hitting another character, for example, makes that punch look much more powerful.

Exaggeration is a useful way to make just that little bit more effort to get a user's attention when you really need it. The animation of the save button used on **CodePen.io** is an example of this (see Figure 2.15). The extravagant movement of the save button makes great efforts to get your attention and remind you to save your work.

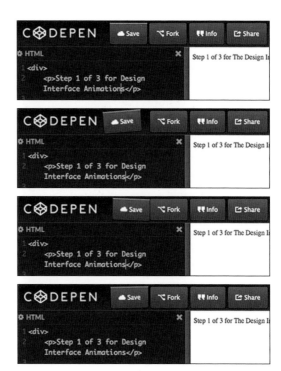

FIGURE 2.15
CodePen's exaggerated motion of the save button reminds you to save your work as you go. You can see it in action in this video: **https://vimeo .com/162721300**.

Exaggeration can also be used to create hierarchy in a group of animations. The most exaggerated motion will be the most powerful and attention-grabbing animation. The more it contrasts with the rest of the animations used, the more exaggerated it will seem.

Achieving exaggeration in code comes down to making the action bigger than you might have done normally. Sometimes, when you see interface animation that you think is overdone or just a bit too much, it's because that animation has been exaggerated more than the context calls for.

Solid Drawing

Solid drawing is the concept of making sure that forms feel as if they are drawn in three-dimensional space, meaning that they are drawn in a way that gives them the appearance of having proper volume, weight, and balance. Most interfaces aren't in true 3D space, at least not right now, but the way you draw an object can hint at what sort of mass or volume it has. Gradients and shadows can suggest a 2D object is rounded, or heavy, or close to a light source or other object. There is a lot of potential power of suggestion in the way an animated element is drawn.

This principle becomes even more applicable when you're working in 3D. It's well beyond the scope of this book to get into the details of things like shading and textures, but one key point that is useful even if you never work in true 3D is the idea that in 3D space (or implied 3D space) smaller objects appear to be farther way. If you're trying to create some depth between the layers of your animation, making the objects that are meant to be farther away smaller will make the overall effect feel much more realistic.

These next few principles may not come up as often in your daily work, but they are still helpful and likely to come in handy sometimes.

Straight Ahead and Pose to Pose

This principle focuses on two different ways of drawing or planning animation. Straight ahead refers to the technique of drawing each frame of an animation in sequence, one right after the other in the order they would play. Pose to pose is the technique of drawing the extremes of the action to establish the main points the action will hit first, and then filling in the in-between frames. (This is where the term *tweening* comes from in animation.)

When you're creating an animation by defining keyframes, like in CSS, for example, you're working in the pose-to-pose style. You define the key extremes of an animation, such as where it starts, the specific stops or property changes it hits along the way, and where it ends. Then, when you preview it in your browser, the rendering engine fills in all the in-betweens for you. It decides what needs to happen to the animating object in between the keyframes you've defined to get it to where it needs to be. This works out really well for predictable animation where there aren't a lot of intricate changes made from one keyframe to the next.

Straight ahead drawing comes into play when you have more unpredictable things to animate, like smoke or drops of water. For things like that, it might be easier to draw each individual frame of the animation to get the effect you want. All sprite-based animations (like the Twitter "like" heart animation) are using this straight ahead drawing style. With animation sprites, each frame is drawn out and placed in order to be played back like a film strip.

At any given time, you may be working in one of these two manners while you animate interface elements, even if you're not actually drawing the frames in the traditional sense. Also, your current tools allow you to blur the lines between these two approaches. Highly dynamic programmatic animations, for example, can be both or neither of these approaches all at the same time.

Appeal

Appeal is the classic principle that is hardest to describe. It's one of those you just know when you see it. Appeal is what makes a character or object in an animation interesting— what draws you to it and makes it appealing to watch or look at. The way you design the items you'll be animating can add to their appeal. Dynamic design can also boost appeal. Interesting shapes, dynamic proportions, and simplicity in design can all add to the visual appeal of an object, even when it's not a cartoon character.

Essentially, there is no one way to guarantee having appeal or a set of steps to follow to get there. In interface animation, good thoughtful design and animation that fits well into its surroundings tends to be more likely to have appeal in an interface. In character animation, appeal is often the way a character makes itself stand out, but standing out too much is often a negative thing for interface animations. In a way, you could say that the most appealing interface animations are the ones that blend so well with the surrounding design and task at hand that they seem invisible at first glance.

Staging

The principle of staging is the most general of all the principles. The very definition of staging is to present every idea in such a way that it is "completely and unmistakably clear." In the classic text, and most animation discussions, this focuses on the storytelling aspect of staging. Storytelling isn't always something that applies to interface animations, but the idea of making sure that the main action is clear certainly is. Animations are often made up of multiple moving parts. Staging as applied to interface animation means being sure that the most important aspect of the animation is clear and stands out among any other design elements. Hopefully, in most cases, this kind of logical hierarchy is already in place with a good layout and design sense in the interface to begin with.

Developing an Eye for Animation

Being familiar with the 12 principles we've just covered gives you a good foundation for judging animation that you encounter and developing an eye for what good animation looks like. The more you look for these individual principles in the animation you see—whether it's in an app, a motion graphics piece, or in animated film—the more easily you'll be able to apply them to your own work.

Look for styles of animation that resonate the most with you, or for the projects you're working on, and identify which principles they use most often and how. **Vimeo.com** is a great site for finding high-quality motion graphics and animations work; look in their staff picks and other design channels. The more you can practice implementing these principles in your tool of choice, the better you'll get at them, and the move intuitive you'll find animating with them becomes.

Recommended Traditional Animation Reads

I find the history and craft of traditional animation to be a fascinating subject to read about. Even when the lessons aren't immediately applicable to the way we work today, the stories are engaging. If you're interested in learning more about the history and tradition of animation, I recommend these four books as a great place to start:

The Illusion of Life
Frank Thomas and Ollie Johnston

This book is the source of the 12 principles of animation and so much more. It contains the story of how early Disney animators changed the face of animation. It's a fascinating story and worth the effort it takes to get your hands on a copy.

The Animator's Survival Kit
Richard Williams

This book focuses entirely on classic animation techniques. It was written after *The Illusion of Life* and some of the concepts have matured or are explained differently here. It's full of helpful animation tips and interesting history lessons as well.

Timing for Animation, 2nd Edition
John Halas and Harold Whitaker

This book is dedicated entirely to timing and how to do it well in animation. It would be impossible not to gain a higher appreciation for timing after reading this book!

The Principles of Animation
Pixar's John Lasseter

The scanned format of this one can be tough to read, but it's a great read on the principles of animation in application.

https://www.cs.cmu.edu/afs/cs/academic/class/15462-f09
/www/lec/Lesseter.pdf.

Staying on Point

Regarding the 12 classic principles of animation, the ones that are the most useful for digital work are:

- Timing and spacing
- Follow-through and overlapping action
- Anticipation
- Secondary action
- Arcs

Modern Principles of Interactive Animation

The classic principles of animation teach us so much about creating natural and pleasing animation, but they fall short in guiding us in one particular area: interactive animations. It's not their fault, of course, because they were written for a different era of animation when interaction wasn't a thing to consider.

Designing interactive animation—which interface animations often are—requires approaching animation just a little differently and working with a different set of rules for behavior. The way your animations behave during an interaction affects how your users perceive them just as much as how they look. The core of what the 12 principles cover still applies to your work, but you also have to consider the interactive context of your work. Your work won't just be watched in the classic definition of animation (like feature films and cartoons); it will be interacted with, too. And that means you have to consider factors beyond the classic principles, or any other motion graphics techniques, when designing quality interface animations.

This chapter covers the principles of interactive animation: the factors that ensure that animations work with the expectations that come with interaction, not against them.

Interactive animation is judged both on how it behaves or responds as well as how it looks. The following principles of interactive animation are guidelines for designing animations that will always work with your users and never get in their way.

Have a Known Purpose

The very first rule of interface animation is that all interface animations must have a purpose for being there. The purpose of a particular animation might be drawn from the UX issue it's intended to help solve, such as, "to draw the user's eye to the change in the items status." An animation's purpose can be as simple as "to communicate the mood and personality of your brand." The only purpose I'd say isn't allowed is "delight" all on its own. Delight isn't something that can be created by animation alone. An animation you add solely to increase delight usually does exactly the opposite from the user's perspective.

All UI animations need to have a defined purpose tied to a design outcome. (Part II of this book covers how to identify an animation's purpose in detail.) If it can't be justified in terms of a design goal, it's probably not worth having there at all.

Don't Create Obstacles

Animation shouldn't get in the way of your user accomplishing the task at hand. Of course, you would never intentionally make it more difficult for your users to complete a given task, but it's easy to get carried away while designing something beautiful. Unfortunately, what you might end up with instead is actually a beautiful obstacle. If at any time your user finds herself waiting unnecessarily for an animation to finish before she can make her next move, there's a problem.

Loaders and instances where data is being fetched or processed are exempt from this rule, of course. There are times when waiting can't be avoided. This rule applies to interactions that can reasonably expect a near immediate response. Animations should never belabor these interactions unnecessarily.

Avoid Animation That Becomes an Obstacle

Square's former site has a fitting example of unintentionally creating obstacles with animation (see Figure 3.1). The main navigation is housed in a full-screen modal, which in itself isn't necessarily a problem. But this modal also has a multistep animated transition that plays out each time it is opened. A dark blue overlay fades in, the lighter blue navigation container stretches out from the middle, and then the list of navigation options slide-fades into view. (You can see it in action in this video: https://vimeo.com/162713180.) That three-step transition takes slightly less than a full second, which doesn't sound like much. But when you realize that every time a user wants to access the main navigation, he'll have to wait through that transition before making a selection—then suddenly navigating through this site becomes a very time-consuming task.

The trouble is that the transition adds time to something that will be accessed often, and the effect used actually makes the task take noticeably longer. Navigation isn't a task that should be slowed down since it's used so frequently. The showy entrance also provides unnecessary emphasis to the navigation opening. Accessing the main navigation should be quick and easy.

There's nothing wrong with the way the animation is designed. It's well done, but a poor match for the content and task at hand. If this same entrance animation were used for something that

FIGURE 3.1
Square's former main menu design. This three-stage transition to access the main navigation is an example of animation becoming an obstacle in an interface. (The site has since been updated with a redesigned navigation that is much less cumbersome for users.)

was accessed more occasionally, like modal windows or a product detail view, it wouldn't be an issue. The showy entrance would help reinforce the importance of the modal message, and the fact that it would only be seen occasionally would help make the content it introduces feel important.

What to Aim for: Animation That Stays Out of the Way

Navigation is a great place to employ animation if it's done in a way that fits the task of navigating a site. For example, the Nixon Watches site has a large amount of navigation and a lot of animation (see Figure 3.2). However, they've used it in a way that doesn't create obstacles or get in your way as a user.

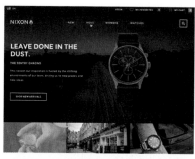

FIGURE 3.2

Nixon's site has a highly animated navigation that avoids creating obstacles by being well-timed and responsive to user input. Check out this video for a closer look: https://vimeo.com/162713179.

Each time you access the navigation, the submenu quickly slides down into place from the top of the screen. It gets out of your way, easily sliding back up to the top of the screen when you're done with it as well. Even the entrance of new submenus when you select a different top-level menu item is animated with the same snappy slide-in movement. Despite all the animation that's happening, it's not creating an obstacle between you and the task you are trying to complete.

When you're animating something as critical as navigation, you want the animations you design to be more like the ones on Nixon Watches' menu—animations that pair well with the content at hand and don't make users wait for them. The animation gets quickly to the point, without extra flourish or taking unnecessary amounts of time.

Keep Animations Flexible

Sometimes animation and interaction find themselves at odds. Animation is generally linear in nature—it has a specific set of states or frames to play through from start to end, and some amount of time must pass for that to happen. Interaction, on the other hand, is nonlinear. Users can click, scroll, swipe, or otherwise offer other sorts of input at any time. Even when an animation is only a fraction of a second long, it's still possible for some input to occur during that time. And that's where things can get tricky.

Good interface animations need to be flexible and always feel responsive to a user's input even if the animation is currently animating. Think of it like a conversation. The best conversations are ones where you feel as if the other person is listening to you and responding to what you've said. If they're nonresponsive or don't seem to be paying attention, you're less likely to trust their responses or continue conversing with them. The same goes for interfaces. If a user starts to realize her input is being skipped or ignored, trust is lost, and the quality of her experience starts to degrade.

An animation that ignores input while it is active is a *blocking animation*, which means that it blocks the user from using it for its intended task while it's animating. An animation that responds to input even while it's actively animating is *nonblocking*. You should always aim to create nonblocking animation unless there is a compelling reason not to do so, because blocking behavior can make the interface feel broken or slow when it doesn't respond as expected. The difference between blocking and nonblocking animation is easier to show than describe, so let's look at an example of each.

The Bad: Blocking Animation

Once you see blocking animation in action, you'll start noticing it everywhere. It's quite common on the web, despite its negative impact on the overall user experience. While their site does many things right, Mammoth Booth's navigation is a good example of blocking animation (see Figure 3.3). When you select a page from their main navigation, say the FAQ page, the between page transition starts behind the scenes. If you click on a different page, Gallery, for example, before the FAQ page has finished transitioning in, your second click is ignored. The page that transitions into view isn't the Gallery page, even though that's the one you're expecting, because it's the last navigation item you clicked. Instead, you see the FAQ page, which was the first one you clicked, and the only one of your clicks that the site responded to. All other input was ignored once that page transition was initiated. That's blocking animation in action.

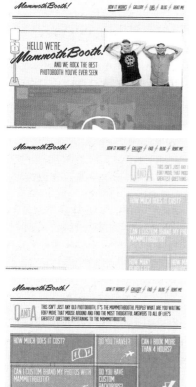

FIGURE 3.3

The Mammoth Booth site's blocking animation behavior: it loads the FAQ page because no user input is accepted during the page transitions. See it in action in the video version here: https://vimeo.com/162713178.

Sometimes, menu items or buttons are visually disabled while page transitions or other transitions are occurring, in order to reduce logic complexity. But this isn't actually a better solution. It does prevent the possibility of the user realizing his input is being ignored, but it also exaggerates the blocking behavior of the animation and doesn't solve the core issue.

The best solution is to design and build your interface animations so they are interruptible and don't block input—build them to both accept and respond to user input, no matter where in their animated action they currently are. Interruptible animations are nonblocking animations.

In Mammoth Booth's case, only small changes would be necessary for the animation to be interruptible and nonblocking. The transition to the FAQ page could have been stopped when the Gallery link was clicked and then started the transition to the Gallery page instead. Or, even better, the page transition could have adapted to its new destination of the Gallery page mid-transition. With either solution, you would have gotten the response you expected, and the experience would have been much improved.

What to Aim for: Nonblocking Animation

Stripe Checkout has a good example of nonblocking animation in its checkout flow (see Figure 3.4). When you check the "Remember me everywhere" box, some additional information and a form field fold down into place. When you uncheck the box, they fold right back up out of sight. If you change your mind and deselect the box before the fold-down animation completes, it interrupts itself mid-animation and moves directly into folding back up, reversing its direction in an instant when you change your selection. It doesn't matter how fast or how many times you check and uncheck that box, the animation is working with you and responding to your input the whole way through. It's a well-executed nonblocking animation. You never have to wait for it to finish, and it can be interrupted at any time.

This nonblocking animation behavior is what you want to aim for in all the animated interactions you design. It may require a little more programming or design logic on your end, but the benefit to your users will be tenfold. The fact that the animation responds to their input, no matter when they give it, makes the interaction the kind

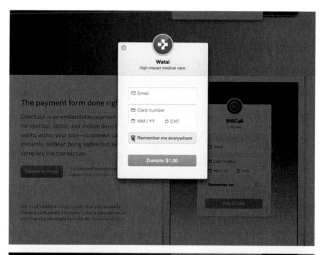

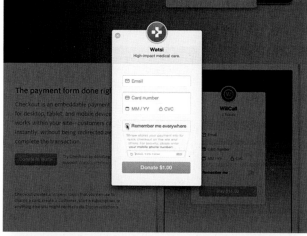

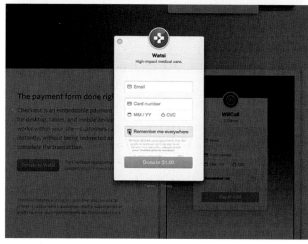

FIGURE 3.4
Stripe Checkout's form animation always responds to user input, even when it's mid-animation. Its nonblocking behavior means it will always respond to user input, no matter what. See the slow motion video version for a closer look: **https://vimeo .com/162713181**.

of conversation that they want to continue. It builds trust by always appearing to be listening to them and by never making users feel like they're being ignored.

> **TIP** NONBLOCKING IS BEST
>
> All animated interactions should be nonblocking by default.

Be Quick, Be Readable: Timing

The classic principles' definition of timing still applies to your work with interactive animation, but your timing decisions exist in a very specific and very different context than the sort of animation the principle was written for. Most people using or interacting with the animations in interfaces are trying to get something done. Whether they're in the midst of completing a specific task, or looking for some specific information, they're on their way to some end goal that's important to them. Your audience isn't sitting back and watching your animations tell a long-form story like the ones the classic principles were written for.

You need to take your user's task-based mindset into consideration when deciding on the timing for your animation work as one additional factor on top of the other timing factors to consider. Often, designers take the context of an interface to mean that all interface animations should always be lightning fast to stay out of the way. Or they look for one specific small number, like 0.30s for example, to use as the duration for all or any interface animations, as a golden rule that can't ever be deviated from. Both those generalizations oversimplify the problem and won't result in high-quality animation. Good timing is more an art than a science. Thinking in terms of guidelines, as opposed to hard-and-fast rules, will serve you much better in your design work.

A Good Range for Interface Animations

Instead of having one set duration for all your interface animations, aim to keep them within the range of 200ms–500ms (see Figure 3.5). Small UI transitions that involve smaller elements or small amounts of change tend to be on the lower end in the 200ms to 350ms range. Larger motion that covers a lot of ground or motion that uses complex bounce transitions usually ends up on the higher end of this range, around 400ms to 500ms. There can always be exceptions, of course, but if you stick within this range, you'll be off to a good start.

ADAPTED FROM HTTPS://AEROTWIST.COM/BLOG/FLIP-YOUR-ANIMATIONS/

FIGURE 3.5
Timing windows for UI animations.

The numbers of this range are largely based on research from the Nielsen Norman Group and the Model Human Processor. In their article on the three important limits for response times,[1] the Neilson Norman Group states that 0.1 seconds (or 100ms) is perceived as instant, and 1 second is considered the upper limit of a user's flow of thought. Together, these outline a range of 0.1s to 1s for feedback, animated or otherwise, to feel connected to a specific user action or input. From this research, we can conclude that animations should all be more than 0.1s (100ms) to be perceived at all.

Additionally, the Model Human Processor,[2] a methodology of formal Human-Computer Interaction, states that on average it takes a human 230ms to visually perceive something. This is where the start of the suggested range comes from. An animation with a duration of 200ms will be just within range to be perceived by the average person. Any shorter than that, and you risk it not being visually perceived at all, which would defeat the purpose of animating it in the first place.

The Nielsen Norman Group's response limits article suggests that 1s is the upper limit for animation durations within interfaces. They do note that at 1s, the user will already notice the delay, but still realize

1 Response Times: The 3 Important Limits: http://www.nngroup.com /articles/response-times-3-important-limits/.

2 Model Human Processor: http://rfld.me/1NqupOz.

the response is connected to the previous action. That's why it's the upper limit. You likely won't have lost your users entirely, but they're not going to be happy about how long things are taking. You don't want your interface animations to be perceived as slow or annoying, so that's why the suggested upper limit for interface animation durations is 500ms (or 0.5s).

More Complex Easing Needs More Time to Be Readable

It's generally easy to notice that large motions or animating big changes need longer durations. Moving a modal box across the screen as it exits from view will obviously need more time to complete its action than a button's background color animating to show its active state. In the same way, animation that uses complex easing also tends to need longer durations to be readable. The direction changes found in bounce or elastic easing present more visual information to parse, and that takes more time to be "read" or understood (see Figure 3.6). It may only need 20ms–30ms more, but that can make all the difference between an animation that looks "broken" and one that looks like it bounces.

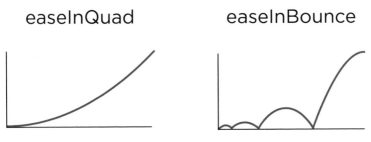

easeInQuad   easeInBounce

FIGURE 3.6
Visually parsing the more complex motion that will result from the easeInBounce above will likely require more time than the more simplistic easeInQuad curve. (Both these curves and their associated code can be found on **easings.net**.)

Readability should be your standard for judging the timing of your interface animations, instead of one single duration that's used for all animation. Stop reducing the duration of an animation for the sake of speed as soon as you hit the point where it no longer communicates what it's supposed to. If you can no longer tell what the motion is supposed to be, its duration has been made too short.

Focus on How the Animation Feels to Interact With

Keeping with the metaphor of good interactions being a lot like good conversations, interface animations' timing should always feel good to interact with. The only way to judge this is to try the animation out for yourself. Or even better, have others try it, too. It's often difficult to judge the timing of your own animation objectively, so an outside opinion can be very helpful.

If an animation feels right, even though it has a duration of 600ms, which is technically outside of the recommended range, go with your gut (or your user research) over the numbers. Designing animations that feel right is more important than following guidelines to a T. Your users will notice how the animations in your interface feel, not any specific numbers of the durations or other factors. They aren't counting the milliseconds.

The more animation experience you gain, the better your timing instincts will become. You'll start picking durations that feel right sooner and develop your own rules of thumb for animating. Timing is more of an art than a science. The more you do it, the better you'll be at it. That's just one more reason why prototyping and practice is so important for designing interface animations.

Performance Matters

Performance is not mentioned at all in the classic principles. It's not something that classic animators had to consider in the same sense that we do, so it never came up. There's no need to consider how the host technology might impact the experience of your animations when they are all prerendered frames on film. On the web, however, performance is hugely important. Animations that are slow and sluggish to interact with won't have a positive impact on the user experience, no matter how well they are designed. Poor performance negates even the most carefully considered experience. That's why it is so important to consider performance early and often throughout your animation design process.

Sometimes, you intentionally push the limits of your technology, but other times, performance issues come up when you least expect it. There are other books out there that cover this topic in great technical detail (like Lara Hogan's *Designing for Performance*: http://designingforperformance.com/), but here is a short list of considerations to help you make the most performant design decisions you can while you're designing and planning your animation efforts.

Animate the Most Efficient Properties

Whether you are animating in CSS or JavaScript, you're affecting specific properties of the element you're animating. Browsers can animate some properties more efficiently than others, based on how many steps need to happen behind the scenes to update said property.

Browsers are particularly efficient at animating opacity, scale, rotation, and position (when done with transforms). See this article from Paul Irish and Paul Lewis for the details on why these are the most performant properties to animate.[3] Conveniently, these are also the most common properties that designers want to animate. There aren't many animated effects that can't be pulled off with this list, even though it's short. Stick to these properties to set your animations up for the best performance results from the start. If you find yourself needing to animate a property outside of this list, check **csstriggers.com** to find out how much of an additional impact it might have on performance.

> **TIP** MOST PERFORMANT PROPERTIES
>
> To get the best performance out of CSS animations, stick to these properties:
>
> - Opacity
> - Scale
> - Rotation
> - Position (when done with transforms)

---

3 High Performance Animations by Paul Irish and Paul Lewis: http://www.html5rocks.com/en/tutorials/speed/high-performance-animations/.

Use the Tools That Fit What You Need

One of the biggest advantages of the current web animation landscape is the range of tools we have at our disposal. We can use CSS animations and transitions to add just a dash of interface animation to our work, or go all out with WebGL to create a full 3D experience, all within our browser. Having this huge range of options is wonderful, but it also means you need to be cognizant of what you're using to get the job done.

Loading in the full weight of a robust JavaScript animation library is overkill if you're only animating a few small elements here and there. That extra overhead will have an impact on performance. Try to match the complexity of the technology you choose to the complexity of your animation needs to avoid unnecessary performance strain.

For small amounts of animation on the web, stick to CSS solutions since it's the lightest option out there. As your animations grow in complexity and the need for deeper logic, move to JavaScript solutions that can accomplish what you need.

Always keep an eye on how much you are loading in versus what you're actually using. If you're only employing 10% of your chosen animation library in your work, that's a good time to look for a lighter more efficient solution or maybe even create a custom solution that only does exactly what you require.

Use Offsets to Lighten the Load of Animating Many Things

Offsets—the concept of having a series of similar movements execute one slightly after the other, creating a wave-like pattern—are a long-held motion graphics trick for creating more interesting and organic motion. Employing this trick of the trade can also be smart for performance. Animating a large number of objects at once can put a strain on the browser's rendering abilities. Adding delays to offset these animations in time, so they no longer all start at the same time, can impact the rendering performance positively. It's a happy coincidence that this motion graphics trick can benefit performance, too.

Perceived Performance: Animation Can Make Your Interface Feel Faster

This is the other side of the performance coin, if you will. Making sure that what you design will be performant in the browser is the most common focus of performance conversations, but *perceived* performance is another aspect of performance where animation can have an impact on your users. Animation alone can't make your interface faster, but it can help fill in unavoidable gaps and create the perception that things are happening faster. Or at the very least, it can reassure users that something is, in fact, happening behind the scenes.

Discussions of performance are often centered around the goal of attaining 60 frames per second for any animation on-screen. This can be a helpful benchmark for testing and other data-centric investigation, but it's not a goal your audience will notice specifically. In fact, they don't care at all what the fps is, as long as nothing looks broken and things feel like they're working well. Perceived performance is harder to measure because it is less concrete than fps, but it is often the best benchmark to use, because the difference between 50fps and 60fps may not be perceivable to your audiences in the context of your project or the task at hand.

That wraps up the principles of interactive animation. It's a short list, but an important one. When you combine these with an appreciation for the classic animation principles, you'll be creating interface animation that is both beautiful and pleasant to interact with. That combination will make your animation work stand out.

Staying on Point

To design animation that is as pleasant to interact with as it is beautiful, remember:

- Have a known purpose for every animation in your interface.

- Don't create obstacles with animation.

- Keep animations flexible and nonblocking.

- Focus on readability above duration.

- Animate the most performant CSS properties to set yourself up for good performance from the start.

PART II

Using Animation to Solve Design Problems

The best interface animations have both purpose and style. They must have a functional reason for being there, and they have to look good and communicate well while doing it. I like to call interface animations with a balanced combination of purpose and style *invisible animation*. Like the concept of invisible design, invisible interface animations are so well done, so seamlessly part of the interaction, that you don't even notice that you're looking at animation. When you design animations that are so good they just become part of the interface like a true team player, that's a job well done!

Purpose and style are both equally necessary for invisible interface animation. An animation with a perfectly good purpose for being there will be undermined and ineffective if its look and behavior are lacking. On the other hand, a beautifully executed animation that has no functional reason for being there will undermine its beauty by being annoying and distracting.

In the last two chapters, we focused on the style side of the equation. Understanding the classic principles of animation and developing motion design skills help us make sure our animations look appealing and express the qualities we want them to express. Put another way, the style half of the equation is the visual design side of animation. The purpose side of the equation is equally important, and that's what this next section focuses on.

Knowing that animation can provide benefits when used well is great. But where exactly can it help? And how do we find the right places to put it? Those are the questions this section will answer. Each chapter in this section identifies a common design problem or task that animation can potentially help with, along with examples for each. As with many design methods, these are often used in combination. Feel free to choose which one (or ones) might best serve you in your upcoming projects while reading through this section.

CHAPTER 4

Using Animation to Orient and Give Context

A nimation has the power to suggest space and movement in ways that none of your other design tools really can. This makes it especially useful for helping to communicate the lay of the land in your screen-based interfaces through visual hints and special suggestions. It also has the power to suggest depth and space, two things we encounter regularly in the physical world but are often difficult to replicate on-screen.

Motion can be used to suggest boundaries, layers, and hint at what lies beyond the edges of what's visible on-screen. Even a small visual clue can make understanding the landscape of an interface easier to understand at a glance, saving time and effort to explain which objects are located where. Think of it like a mime drawing the outline of an invisible door. With one gesture, the entire audience knows exactly where the imaginary door is and why the mime can't walk through it, even though none of them can see it. A shared understanding has been created between the audience and the mime. Motion in an interface can accomplish the same results.

Create a Mental Model of What's Out of View

When you're trying to fit a large amount of content into a small amount of space, it gets really hard to fit everything on-screen. Actually, it's impossible. If you've ever worked on a responsive design or anything that considers the smallest viewport sizes, you know that fact well. Even when you can fit everything on-screen at once, it's rarely an ideal solution for the design for the experience.

Patterns like off-screen navigation or interfaces that exist in layers— some stacked behind or in front of what's currently in view—have emerged to help fit a lot of information into a small space in a meaningful way. Using animation to transition between layers or bring off-screen elements into view helps reinforce the spatial relationships of the interface for your users.

Orient Interface Layers with Animation

Wacom's navigation is a great example of using motion to orient users to the layers of an interface (see Figure 4.1). Initially, when you load the site, only the top layer (and top level) of the navigation is visible. But once you hover over one of the menu items, the top layer slides out of the way to reveal the submenu behind it. That little bit of animation—the fact that you actually see the main navigation shrink out of the way—is what gives that visual cue that the subnavigation is on a layer behind it.

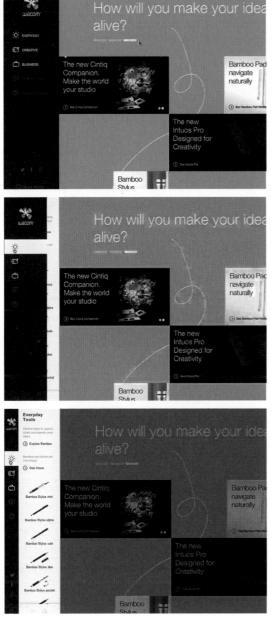

FIGURE 4.1
Frame by frame of the Wacom navigation layers. The main navigation animates out of the way to reveal the submenu on the layer below. The video version shows it in action as well: **https://vimeo .com/162715956.**

If the animation were removed, the interaction wouldn't break, but it would be more difficult to understand what happened. A hard cut from a wide main menu to a skinny main menu with the subnavigation showing next to it would have given users access to the same set of options, but it would also be disorienting. Where did this white menu come from? How did I get to it? Where did the dark gray menu go? With no animated transition between these states, the users would be left to decipher the answers for themselves.

The presence of the animated transitions saves you from wondering about those questions by visually showing the spatial and hierarchical relationship between the menus on the screen. Cognitive load has been reduced because users don't have to think up a spatial model of their own or spend energy thinking about how or why the menu changed shape. Thanks to the animation, they now know where the subnavigation is and where it can be found again. The model of how the menu objects are related in space has been revealed to them in a way that requires no more effort than to observe the movement on-screen. Their brainpower is saved for more important tasks.

By observing this one transitional animation, users have also started creating the mental model of the layers in the interface and which information lives on which layer level. It will take more than just one animation to really cement this mental model in their minds, of course. Once you've introduced a certain spatial arrangement of elements into your design, it's up to you to make sure that you are consistent with the spatial relationships you set up throughout your design to keep these models true.

Splitting an interface into layers is another common approach for handling large quantities of information. Different contexts, different content, or different tasks may be relegated to specific layers to keep their differences clear. Layers are often used in interfaces to house different kinds of information. All modals, for example, can exist on a higher layer than the main content of a site like the sign-up modal shown in Figure 4.2 on Shopify.com.

When a modal is opened, the modal content moves toward the viewer, indicating a move to a higher layer that exists above the current page. When you close the modal, its exit animation makes it appear to sink back down a level, returning to you the main content layer.

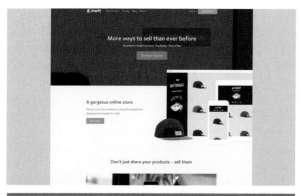

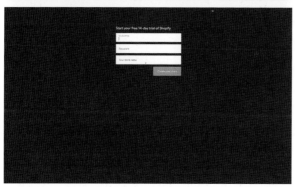

FIGURE 4.2

Shopify's sign-up modal gets larger as it fades in to create the effect that it's moving closer to you and moving up to a layer above the main content. You can see the modal in action in this video: **https://vimeo .com/162715955.**

Another example of this layered technique is on **Leapsecond2015.com** (see Figure 4.3). They take this metaphor of modals existing one layer above the content even further by moving their content backward in space while the modal moves forward. They effectively exaggerate the movement and the space between layers and imply an even greater distance between the two layers.

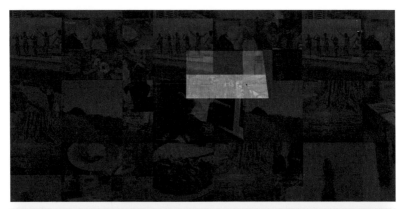

FIGURE 4.3
Leapsecond2015's modal video player exists on a layer above the main content. The main content moves backward in space while the opening modal moves forward in space to show the difference and distance between these two layers. See full motion in the video version: **https://vimeo.com/162715959.**

Interestingly, **leapsecond2015.com**'s movement is created in actual 3D space (created with three.js), whereas Shopify's animation is a scaled movement that only suggests 3D. As a user, you still get the implied movement between layers with both animations, even though the execution is different. It's interesting to note that true 3D is not required for the suggestion of 3D space to be understood.

In both examples, the visible movement to a higher layer helps to differentiate the kind of content and the kind of interaction required at each layer level. For Shopify, the higher layer that the modals occupy is a space that requires information and decisions from the user, while the lower layer provides information about Shopify itself. In Leap Second 2015, the modal layer is for watching videos, and the main layer is for selecting videos.

Animating the movement between layers serves to make the layer change more apparent and establish the separate layers as their own space, much like they would be if they were physical objects layered on top of each other. Movement is required to change the layer order of objects in the physical world. Animated layer transitions use that metaphor to create a shared understanding of space. It's a very effective technique to establish layers within an interface, even when the layering is more complex and more than two layers are used.

Orient the User to Off-Screen Objects with Animation

Off-screen patterns have become more common as devices and screens have gotten smaller. On the web, this is very often used for off-screen navigation patterns or similar patterns that keep a section of content waiting just outside the viewable screen area for when it's needed. This approach is best for content that is global in scope and important enough to be needed by the user at any time, which is why it's used so often for navigation and the like.

Cotton Bureau has a good example of this on its site, as shown in Figure 4.4. Both their shopping cart and navigation are off-screen elements that transition into view with a tap of their respective buttons. The animation of both the content moving into view from the side, as well as the main content sliding along with it to make room, reinforces the model that the content is waiting in the wings. The navigation is always off to the left side, and the shopping cart is always off to the right side.

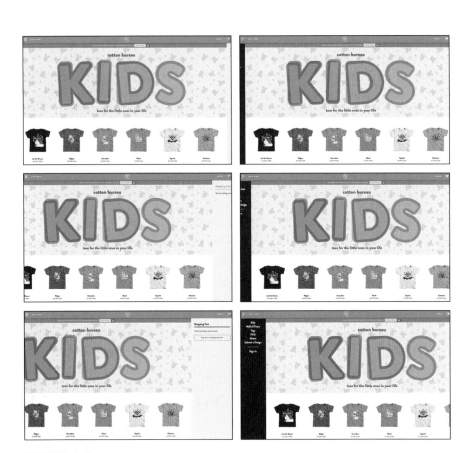

FIGURE 4.4
Cotton Bureau animates its off-screen navigation and shopping cart in and out of view to reinforce visually where they are located and where they can be found again. See it in action in the video version:
https://vimeo.com/162715960.

Both elements are consistent in the nature of their animation—both move in a straight line pushing the content along with it and always return to the same place they came from. Both also use the same duration and easing for their animation. The direction of the movement reinforces where each came from and where it will return to. A user can quickly form the mental model of the navigation being off the screen to the left and the shopping cart being just out of view on the right. And that model will be consistently reinforced by the design so the user always knows exactly where to find the navigation or shopping cart without having to give it much thought in future interactions.

Guide Tasks

Animation can be extremely helpful for guiding users through linear task flows. Guiding tasks is very similar to the concept of cueing that has been examined in academic studies. Using animation to keep users on task, and to provide a hint to what comes next, can help users complete the task more easily.

The Basecamp 2 and Readme sites use animation to guide users through the task of signing up for their services. Both also use that animation to differentiate their brand by infusing the animation with their brand's personality. In both cases, the animation used has two purposes: to guide the task and to convey brand personality.

Basecamp 2 animated a hand-drawn character next to its sign-up form (see Figure 4.5). At first, the character appears to be just an illustration alongside the form. However, once you start filling out the form, the character's arm and pointing finger move to follow the form field that is active. The character's big wide smile changes to a concerned "uh-oh" expression to help indicate that an error has been made in filling out the form.

FIGURE 4.5

A hand-drawn character leads you through the Basecamp 2 sign-up form by pointing to the active field and reacting dramatically to help highlight an error. See full motion in the video version: https://vimeo.com/162715964.

Readme's sign-up form has a character for a similar purpose, and they take the character's personality up a level or two. They use their illustrated owl mascot to almost gamify their sign-up and sign-in forms in a subtle and meaningful way, which is no small feat (see Figure 4.6). Forcing the mascot on-screen could easily have resulted in a distraction or annoyance like Microsoft's infamous Clippy character or worse. But using restraint and staying focused, Readme has managed to avoid that potential pitfall entirely.

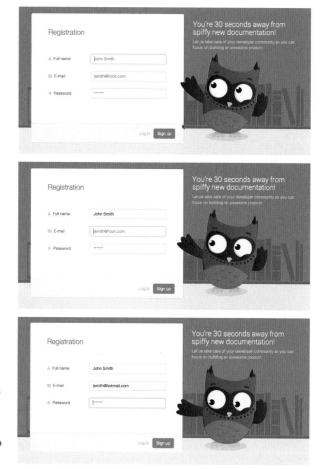

FIGURE 4.6
Readme's owl mascot guides you through the task of signing up for the service by following the active field with animated movements of its eyes and feathers. See full motion in the video version: **https://vimeo .com/162715966**.

On the sign-up form, the owl's eyes and feather hand move to point to the active field throughout the form filling process. After your account has been created, the owl returns on the sign-in form where it covers its eyes when you get to the password field (see Figure 4.7).

The animated owl has more utility on the sign-up form by helping to keep your focus on the currently active form field. Having it appear on the sign-in form as well reminds you of that experience and re-enforces the playful personality of Readme's brand. Any time you can combine both a fitting amount of utility and an equally fitting amount of brand personality to an animation, you've made a very effective design choice!

FIGURE 4.7
Readme's owl mascot returns to the sign-in page where it covers its eyes when the password field is active. See full motion in the video version: **https://vimeo .com/162923170.**

In both the Basecamp 2 and Readme examples, the animated character is not the only thing that indicates the user's current place in the form. Both also leave the focus outline on the form field as you tab or click to the next field. This means that any nonsighted user, or anyone using assistive technology, will still get the default browser-level information about which form field is active. The redundancy used in the design makes it more universal and provides a back-up indication of this important information. It's also a great example of using animation as progressive enhancement.

Inform Context Changes

Any time the view of the content on-screen changes—switching to a detailed view, zooming in, reordering a list, etc.—the context of that content has shifted. The context might be shifted to give a more detailed view, or a less detailed view, of the same information. Or it might be changed to reveal new information about that content. Shifting the context can make it easier for users to understand the content they're looking at; however, the way that context change occurs has the potential to be disorienting.

Using animation to visually smooth out and inform context changes can reduce the chances of disorienting users by making the context change play out in plain view and guiding the eye through the shift. Using animation to show where elements have moved to, which elements have newly appeared, and which elements were there all along, make shifts in context easier to follow. When the change can be followed visually, there's less chance of users losing their place and less chance for them to be unsure if what they're looking at is indeed still the same content.

Generally, a context change can be put into one of two categories: a change in context of the content itself—like switching to a more detailed view—or a change of the interaction mode —like switching from input mode to editing mode. Animation can help reduce potential confusion in both of these cases.

Animate Context Changes in Content

Context changes often involve looking at the same content at a different angle, or with different amounts of detail. For example, check out how Sarah Drasner switches from the map marker to the address details in this map demo (see Figure 4.8). The map pin shape animates into the larger box shape before the address details are revealed. Animating this change from pin to detail box visually maintains that this is still the same content; in this case, a specific location, displayed in a different way. Users see the shape change as the pin morphs into the address listing on-screen, and they don't have to work to maintain that connection for themselves. It's easier to follow because it's spelled out visually in front of them.

FIGURE 4.8
In this map example, the pin morphs into the address modal box to show that it's displaying the same location with a different level of detail. You can see the map in action in this video: **https://vimeo .com/162715963.**

The success of this animation is in large part due to the way it was designed and how the motion was chosen. A different kind of animation, say one that faded the map pin out before fading the address box in, would still be animated, but it would not have maintained the connection between the two shapes. It wouldn't have been obvious that the pin turned into the box without that shape-morphing effect. The fact that the animation keeps the main shapes visible on-screen throughout the motion is what makes this visual context connection so strong.

A simpler context shift is handled in a similar way in Basecamp 2's file display section (see Figure 4.9). The connection between the thumbnail and detail view of an uploaded file is maintained with a simple yet well-placed zooming animation. When viewing the current list of files available in the project, you see a list of icons and titles for files that are currently present. Clicking on a file triggers an animation that has the file's icon zoom forward into the detail modal box.

That simple scale animation reinforces the fact that you're looking at the same file, just in a more detailed view. It's as if the file icon hops into the modal to reveal its particulars. The reverse happens when closing the detail view as well. The file icon scales back down to the thumbnail size as the detail modal box closes.

FIGURE 4.9
Basecamp 2's choice of modal animation helps connect the context between the thumbnail view and the detail view of the same file. See full motion in the video version: https://vimeo.com/162715962.

Both these examples also employ the technique of visual persistence. That is, having objects that exist in both views stay on-screen instead of transitioning out of view just to come back in later. The visual persistence of the main objects involved (the black shapes for the map and the file icon for the file view) help to make the context change clearer. Keeping the main elements visible throughout the context change makes it obvious that they are indeed the same elements. Visual persistence is very useful for showing continuity.

Animate Context Changes in Interactions

Context changes can also involve changing the current interaction mode. In these cases, animating the context change helps make the fact that the current mode of the interface has switched and the purpose of the elements in view has changed.

Take the thumbs-up button to send button animation in Facebook's Messenger app, for example (see Figure 4.10). When you're reading a message thread, the far-right button is a thumbs-up icon that you can tap to send a quick response. However, as soon as you start typing a response, that icon morphs into a send button to indicate you've left the quick response mode and are now typing a full text response. The purpose of that button has changed from a quick response trigger to a text message-sending button, and the morphing animation is used to indicate that change to the user.

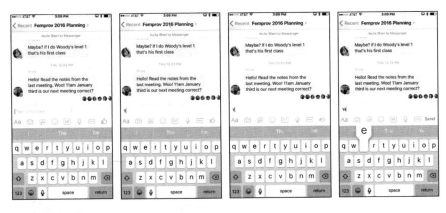

FIGURE 4.10

The shape morph between the thumbs-up button and the send button in Facebook Messenger helps indicate the context change between message-sending modes. See the video version: **https://vimeo.com/162715965.**

Gumroad uses animation to help indicate the functional change between checking out with PayPal and checking out with your credit card (see Figure 4.11). The checkout flow changes based on which payment option you opt to use, and that change is indicated with a short 3D card flip animation. On one side of the card is the credit card payment form, and on the other is a prompt for your PayPal email address to start off the PayPal payment flow.

FIGURE 4.11

The 3D flip transition between the credit card payment method and the PayPal payment method options helps reinforce that both form sections are used for the same purpose via different paths. See it in action in this video: **https://vimeo.com/162715967**.

Having only one of these form sections visible at once helps to ensure that users only enter the payment info they actually need for the option they've selected. And having them flip to occupy the same part of the form, without leaving the page or triggering a reload of information, makes it clear that they both accomplish the same purpose. The either/or choice is made even more evident by the type of animation they choose to use. It's almost literally a coin toss. The fact that they occupy the same space also saves time in having to visually rescan the form to find your place after the change. Gumroad has designed both sections to be as brief as possible, which is an added bonus here as well. Good animation can never make up for poor design, but it can absolutely enhance good design decisions and make them even better.

We've looked at just a handful of examples of using animation to help orient users to your interfaces and how animation can inform content relationships. There are many other examples of this out there, too. You'll notice more and more of them now that you know what to look for. Keep these examples, and others you see, in mind for your own work. When you find yourself needing to show where objects exist out of view or better illustrate the relationship between multiple views or multiple pieces of content, using animation can help you get there.

Staying on Point

Animation can help orient users to the spatial relationships in your interface. It's especially helpful for:

- Helping users create a mental model of the interface, even the parts that aren't currently in view.

- Moving between layers of a layered interface.

- Guiding users through the steps to complete a task.

- Connecting content through context changes.

CHAPTER 5

Using Animation to Direct Focus and Attention

Of all the design tools available to us on the web, animation is the one most likely to be using its outside voice at any given moment. Animation is incredibly useful for attracting attention. In fact, that's a big part of why it's used so much in annoying banner ads. Imagine yourself scrolling through an article on a website and halfway through the article, you find yourself looking at a banner ad with a pixelated dancer pitching you lower mortgage rates. I'm sure it's happened to you, too. Maybe even recently, unless you have an ad blocker installed.

Banners are a big part of why animation on the web has a bad reputation. Nearly all of the web animation we've been exposed to until recently has been poorly executed and has exploited the power of animation to annoy and distract. No wonder there is so much bias against animation on the web!

The main reason that animation in banner ads seems so awful and annoying is that it's preying on our visual reflexes to trick us into paying attention to something that's not important to us. Those animated ads are using animation's power for evil, if you will. But animation's attention-grabbing power can also be used for good. By pairing the visual weight of animation with content that users actually care about, or even information that's most important to them, you can use this often misused aspect of animation for good.

Direct Attention to the Most Important Content

There is usually a short list of things that your users are most interested in reading or accomplishing when they open up your site or app. Pairing animation with that most important thing helps reinforce its importance and makes sure that it's noticed.

Fitbit does this well on its website and iOS app (see Figures 5.1 and 5.2). The number one thing that Fitbit users are interested in when they open up the app or site is their data totals. They want to know if they've burned enough calories to eat that donut guilt-free, or if they need to get more steps in to meet their daily total.

The way animation is used in the dashboard shows that Fitbit knows this goal. The only thing that animates in either the native app or web version of the Fitbit dashboard is the user's data: their statistic totals and the badges to celebrate hitting a goal. Nothing else animates. Not the background bars of the chart. Not even page transitions between viewing different days in the iOS app. The result is a highly animated dashboard, but all the animation is focused on making the most important information on the dashboard easier to take in at a glance.

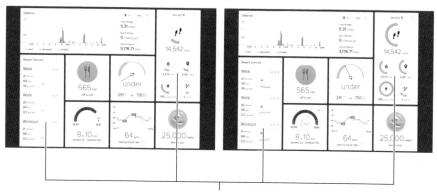

The user data for total steps, distance and the workout heart rate timelines animating in as the dashboard loads.

FIGURE 5.1

The web version of Fitbit's dashboard reserves animation for user data like total steps taken, calories remaining, and sleep tracking. See it in action in the video version: **https://vimeo.com/162719982**.

FIGURE 5.2

Fitbit uses animation with the same focus—only animating user's data—on the iOS app as well. This consistent use of animation helps connect their design across different contexts. See it in action in the video version: **https://vimeo.com/162719983**.

The way they've focused on using animation primarily on one kind of content in this way also gives Fitbit another added advantage. The consistent use of animation across the website version and iOS version of the dashboard ties them together. Opening up the iOS app for the first time will feel familiar to someone who has only used the web interface before. This consistent approach to animation helps tie the experience together across different contexts.

Another higher contrast example of using animation to focus users' attention on something that's important to them is CodePen's save button (see Figure 5.3). New Pens need to be saved periodically while you're working on them, so you don't lose your work. To remind users of that, the save button starts pulsing after a minute or so of not saving your work. This acts as a reminder to save your in-progress work.

The exaggerated nature of the save button's animation could be considered over the top or too much in other contexts. But saving your work is a very important task; the visual volume of the exaggerated motion matches the importance of the task.

FIGURE 5.3

CodePen.io uses an exaggerated wobble animation on the save button to get your attention when you have unsaved work. See it in action in the video version: **https://vimeo .com/162721300.**

The amount of the animation used for an interaction should match the size of the task.

Direct the Eye with Motion

You can take catching the eye with animation one step further by using the direction of the motion to indicate where the user should look next—essentially, guiding the eye through the hierarchy of content using motion. Pinterest does this well with the animations used in the Pin saving micro interactions.

When you click the "Pin it" button for an image in Pinterest's grid view, the animated entrance and exit of the details modal helps you keep track of which thumbnail image you selected. The thumbnail image slides into the modal box, and the direction it moves from is based on its position in the grid (see Figure 5.4). An image in the top left will move diagonally (down and to the right) into the modal box as the modal box fades into view, for example. This motion happens in reverse when you close the modal as well. The direction of the animation helps users visually keep track of which Pin they're interacting with as they move between the thumbnail and detail view. It's as if the thumbnail jumps right into the modal box and then back to its original place if the modal is dismissed. The direction of the motion guides the eye back and forth to keep the focus on the thumbnail image.

Pinterest uses the direction of motion to direct the user's gaze to the alert that confirms a pin was saved as well (see Figure 5.5). From the same modal box, if the user chooses to save the image to one of their boards, the modal box exits out the bottom of the screen with a downward motion. Then the confirmation message animates into view, coming from the bottom of the screen. This is exactly where the user's gaze is focused after following the downward motion of the modal box's exit. Starting the second animation from the same location that the first one ended makes it easier for the user to follow the information flow as it occurs.

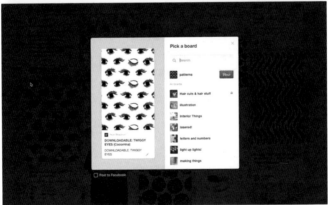

FIGURE 5.4
Pinterest's images move directionally in and out of the modal window based on their position in the grid. You can see it in action in this video: **https://vimeo.com/162719984**.

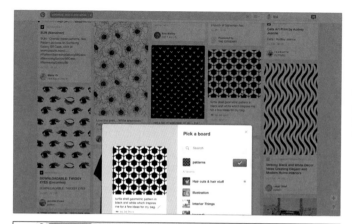

The main modal exits out toward the bottom of the screen.

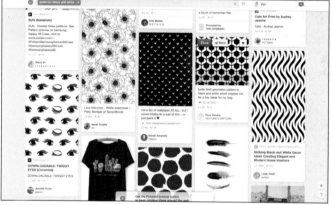

The confirmation messages enter from where the modal left.

FIGURE 5.5

The animation of the alert messages originates from the bottom of the screen—the same place that the modal before it animated to—to guide the eye from one motion to the next. You can see it in action in this video: **https://vimeo.com/162719984**.

Think Eye Flow

The motion graphics industry calls this concept of guiding the gaze from one movement to the next *eye flow*. Considering eye flow is beneficial for animating interfaces as well. Thinking about where the visual focus is likely to be at the beginning and end of a motion helps you design sequences of motion that are logical and feel natural to follow with the eye. A logical flow of motion can influence your user's gaze invisibly and make following the flow of information feel almost effortless. On the other hand, motion that seems to come and go from all directions causes tension and confusion; it quickly starts to distract from the task at hand.

Using Animations Across Different User Contexts

The Pinterest animations discussed in this chapter only occur on larger viewports. They change things up a bit on the website for smaller viewports, as well as on the native iOS app. Both smaller viewport options rely more on animating between layers than the use of directional motion used on larger viewports. This makes Pinterest's use of animation across contexts feel less cohesive than, say, Fitbit's from earlier in this chapter, which consistently animates the same objects in the same way on both the website and the iOS app.

It would be impossible for Pinterest to use the same animations on small viewports as it does on larger viewports. There just wouldn't be space on the screen for the motion. And the motion—especially the movement of the thumbnail images into the details modal box—would be less useful when fewer options are presented in that smaller space.

It's likely that you will run into similar issues in your own work. When the amount of screen real estate changes, not every animated solution can scale to fit in a meaningful way. When the exact motion of an animation can't be consistent across all screen size contexts, you can make other aspects of the animations similar, like easing or timing.

Hold Attention with Visual Continuity

During any given transition between two states or two screens, there are three options for the elements involved in the transition: leaving the screen, entering the screen, or the third and often ignored option—staying on-screen.

When elements persist through the transition because they are present in both the beginning and end state, the transition can be easier to follow. That's visual continuity. By keeping that element on-screen—letting that element keep being itself—it's clear that it's the same element it was in the previous state. The only thing that changes is how it's represented over time. Visual continuity makes a transition more semantic; each element is what it is and keeps the same definition of itself throughout the animation.

TIP VISUAL CONTINUITY

Visual continuity means letting an element continue to be itself throughout a transition.

The elements that persist through a transition can be small elements like buttons and icons, or large prominent elements. This approach works equally well for both.

Some transitions need a fresh start, and clearing the screen to repopulate it with predominantly new elements does that well. But when you're transitioning between two closely related states, the clear and restart approach causes connections to be lost. Visual continuity can help you re-enforce that close connection by having a less drastic change between states. Visual continuity means letting an element continue to be what it is throughout a transition.

The Twitter iOS app, for example, used visual continuity in its account-switching interaction in a previous version (see Figure 5.6). When moving from the list view of all saved accounts to the detail view of one account, the account's avatar stays on-screen and moves to its new position at the top while the other accounts' avatars fade out of view.

The benefits of a transition like this are twofold: the way the avatar's animation contrasts with the other objects' animation makes it stand out visually, and the fact that it stays on-screen makes it easy to remember which selection was made. There is no question as to whether or not the avatar image is the same one as in the listing because it stays on-screen. It keeps being itself throughout the transition.

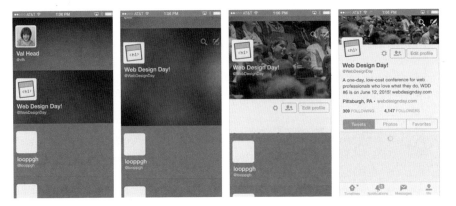

FIGURE 5.6
Visual continuity: the avatar and account name persist on-screen while other elements come and go to complete the transition from account list view to account detail view in the Twitter iOS app. See it in action in the video version: **https://vimeo.com/162719987.**

On a smaller scale, Concrete Matter uses visual continuity well when the site header changes state (see Figure 5.7). The header starts in an expanded full-height state and then compresses into a more compact version as you scroll the page. The icon of its logo moves upward and scales down into its new position in the more compact state. The same end result could have been achieved by fading out the entire large-sized logo and fading the smaller-sized icon into place. But, by keeping the icon in view the whole time, the entire transition is more cohesive and focused.

You know that it's the same icon the whole time because you saw it shrink into its new position. This is a small touch, but it has a big impact on making that state change look and feel more fluid.

Looking for opportunities to use visual continuity will make the transitions you design easier to follow by reducing the potential for visual clutter. It will also make it easier to guide your user's focus through the transition.

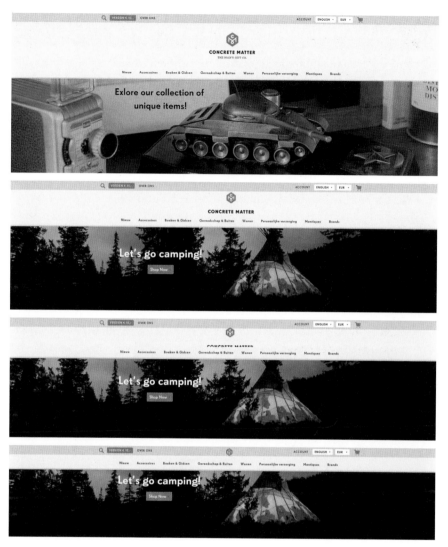

FIGURE 5.7

The visual continuity established by keeping Concrete Matter's logo icon on-screen throughout the transition of the header re-enforces the fact that it's the same logo and header, just displayed differently. See it in action in the video: **https://vimeo.com/162719985**.

Using the attention grabbing power of animation for good can also mean having a little fun with it, too. Focusing on designing animation with purpose doesn't rule out the possibility of fun or delight. It's not for every interaction or every brand, but adding a little surprise in these attention-grabbing moments can be a great opportunity to stand out and connect with your audience.

Zappo's takes advantage of the opportunity to introduce a surprising moment in its iOS app (see Figure 5.8). The otherwise unassuming app has a cat in a cape jump out of the "add to cart" button to add the shoes you're purchasing into the cart icon. To say that animation is unexpected would be an understatement. I doubt that anyone using the Zappos app was expecting a cape-clad cat to appear anywhere at all in the app unless they had prior warning. It's fun, memorable, and just a little bit silly. The animation calls attention to the important action of adding an item to your cart and celebrates the moment with a quick punch of fun.

FIGURE 5.8
Zappos definitely gets a little bit fun and weird when the cat in a cape jumps into your cart. See it in action in this video: **https://vimeo. com/162721302.**

The addition may seem completely random or baseless at first. What do cats in capes have to do with shoes or the Zappos brand? They probably have nothing to do with shoes, but as it turns out, there is a connection to the Zappos brand. One of Zappos' brand pillars is "Create a little fun and weirdness." Fun and weirdness, you say? Check and check. A cat in a cape definitely delivers both!

Attract Attention with Contrast in Animation

Creating contrast by putting an object in motion while it is surrounded by static objects—like the Fitbit dashboard example—is one way to create contrast that draws attention to the object in motion. But a large stark contrast isn't always what the design might call for. More subtle contrast can be created between animated objects by creating contrast in the way that they are animated.

Contrasting Direction of Motion

Contrast can be accomplished by varying direction. Just like a car going the wrong way down a one-way street, moving an element against the established grain will demand attention. If all the animations on a site move from left to right, then one that moves right to left, or up and down will stand out. This change of direction could be useful for denoting that an action has been taken.

The Pinterest modal box discussed earlier in the chapter is an example of this approach. It fades and scales down a layer when dismissed without action, but exits with a downward motion when a pin has been saved. The contrast between action and inaction could be emphasized even more with a modal that exits back to where it came from when dismissed (inaction), and exits in the opposite direction when an action has been taken. This change of direction re-enforces the notion that an action has been taken and something has changed with the contrast of its motion.

Contrasting Easing

Contrast can also be accomplished by varying the style of easing used throughout a collection of animations. Much like you might use a contrasting color in your color palette to denote important content, you can use contrasting easing to do the same.

For example, check out all the modal boxes involved in the ticket-buying process with Tito. The modal box that appears to let you enter payment details for your ticket enters by scaling up into view with a quick ease out easing. Most other modals that you encounter throughout the ticket-buying process use this same style of easing and scaling in, with one exception: the modal alert that appears when you are about to cancel your order.

That modal alert makes its entrance by scaling in with bounce easing. The contrast of this bounce against the measured ease-outs of all the other modals makes this alert stand out even more (see Figure 5.9). The animation works together with the bold red coloring to make it obvious that you are about to take an action that shouldn't be taken lightly.

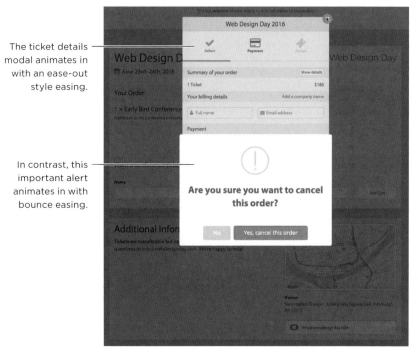

The ticket details modal animates in with an ease-out style easing.

In contrast, this important alert animates in with bounce easing.

FIGURE 5.9
The contrast of the alert message's bounce easing against the regular modal's ease-outs helps to show the weight of the decision and draws attention to the alert. See the video version here: **https://vimeo.com/162719988**.

A contrast of easing is more subtle than a contrast of direction or motion, but it still makes for an effective design detail. The key is creating a palette of easing for your project and using it to create contrast and hierarchy, much like you might do with a color palette. Creating a palette that includes both complementary and contrasting options and using them consistently throughout the design system adds an extra layer of polish and cohesiveness to your design.

We've looked at a few examples of using animation to direct attention by using varying techniques and varying amounts of contrast. Keep an eye out for how the apps and sites you use daily grab attention and create contrast with animation. Do they use it well? Could they be using it more effectively? Now that you know what to look for, you'll start noticing how animation and motion call attention to different objects and actions in the apps and sites you visit regularly. When you find yourself needing to call attention to a specific piece of content or a specific action, consider how you can employ animation to help capture that attention as part of your design system.

Staying on Point

You can use animation's attention grabbing powers for good by:

- Animating the most important content for your users.

- Directing eye flow and guiding the gaze through the content hierarchy with motion.

- Using visual continuity to show when an object hasn't changed.

- Working with a defined easing palette and creating contrast of motion or easing.

CHAPTER 6

Using Animation to Show Cause and Effect

In conversation with other humans (or even with our pets), we rely on subtle cues to know that the other party is listening to us and to judge whether they're still engaged in the conversation. Their facial expressions, how their body is positioned, or in the case of cats, when they just walk away mid-sentence like you aren't even there. All of those small things add up to telling us if the other person is still with us and if we're on the right track.

Interactions with an interface should feel like a good conversation as well, with the interface giving us subtle clues along the way to show it's still listening and guiding us to taking the right actions. Using animation to show the cause and effect of users' actions as they are doing something makes using an interface feel more like an enjoyable conversation.

Showing causality is very much related to the concept of giving feedback, although they are separated in this book because the timing of the information and the kind of information shown for each differs slightly. Cause and effect shows the potential effects of what could happen or what has happened during an interaction. Feedback, on the other hand, lets users know that something has taken place behind the scenes based on their actions.

The need to show cause and effect tends to apply to a very specific subset of interaction types. Apps or sites that have a nonlinear task flow, interactions that require drag and drop or reordering of items, and interfaces that are used to manipulate complex data are among the kinds of interfaces that can benefit the most from revealing causality to their users. By showing causality—the potential effects of an action that's being considered—animation can show the possible results of an action before it's taken, as well as hinting at functionality and exposing affordances.

These hints can act as a guide or cue to help users along a task flow by reinforcing the fact that they are taking the correct action to move forward.

Animation can also be useful for confirming the effect of an action that a user has taken. Confirming what an action made happen is especially important when it's one of many small tasks on the way to completing a larger task.

Guide Tasks by Hinting at Affordances

Affordance is the concept of using an object's characteristics to suggest its functionality and use. Essentially, it's the way an object tells you, via the way it looks or behaves, what you might be able to use it for. The easiest way to remember it is to think of affordances as the possibility of an action that can be taken with an object.

A typical affordance on the web might be adding a gradient to a button so that it appears to be raised, making it more apparent that it can be "pushed" like a real-life button. Animation can be used in similar ways to suggest uses of an object on-screen. This is especially true when the affordances and functionality in question involve gestures. There's really no better way than motion to demonstrate a gesture on screen.

Sometimes these affordance hints can be very subtle, such as Campaign Monitor's email editing tool where the edge of of the top menu pokes in from the left when your cursor gets close to the left edge of the screen (see Figure 6.1). That tiny slide out is just enough of a hint to encourage you to click, and once you do, you've found a new and faster way to return to the top-level menu.

The top layer menu slides out just a few pixels to show you it's there when you move your mouse to the left-hand side of the sidebar.

FIGURE 6.1 Campaign Monitor's email editor animates the edge of the top-layer menu toward you when your cursor hovers near it to show it can be clicked to slide that menu back over the existing one. Using the tool requires a Campaign Monitor account, but you can see it in action in this video as well: **https://vimeo.com/162722219.**

Apple employed a similar (and more easily noticeable) animated hint when the functionality of the camera icon on the iPhone's lock screen changed with an iOS update (see Figure 6.2). (In fact, this hint is still present on the current version of iOS. Try it out for yourself.) When you tap on the camera icon, the whole lock screen animates upward just a few pixels to reveal a hint of the camera's shutter button behind it. The movement hints that you now need to swipe up on the icon, not tap it, to open the camera app. It's extremely effective at conveying the desired behavior even without any explicit instruction. The motion demonstrates a gesture that will open the camera app while also establishing that the camera app persists on a layer behind the lock screen. Two birds with one stone, as they say.

FIGURE 6.2

iOS animates a demonstration of the swipe gesture when you tap the camera icon instead of swiping it. You can see it in action in this video: **https://vimeo.com/162721526**.

The Clear app also uses animation very well to hint at affordances on both the desktop and mobile versions of the app (see Figure 6.3).[1] On the desktop version, as you move your mouse to the bottom of your to-do lists, a new blank list rotates slightly downward from your mouse position to hint that a new list can be created by clicking. If you click to create the new list, but don't enter a name for it, the list block animates out to the left to show that your lack of action (not typing) has caused it to be deleted. That's cause and effect shown well with two simple, yet very well placed, animations.

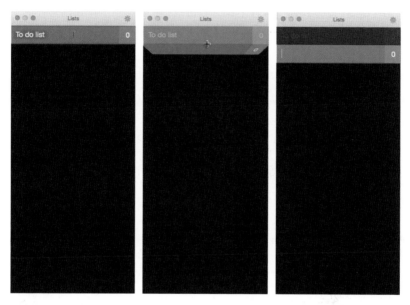

FIGURE 6.3
Clear hints at how to create a new to-do list when your mouse pointer moves to the bottom of your current lists menu. You can see it in action in this video: **https://vimeo.com/162721533**.

Cue by Exposing Additional Actions

Animation can be a very effective way of guiding users through a longer task flow to help them keep their place. By revealing information relevant to the immediate task at hand just as it's needed, you can avoid overwhelming your users with options, while still providing everything they need to complete a series of tasks. Using animation to

---

1 Clear for Mac and iOS from Realmac: **http://realmacsoftware.com/clear/**.

reveal and offer options as they're needed can work to cue users as to what the next step could be based on their recent actions.

Medium uses an animated contextual menu to guide you through writing a story (see Figure 6.4). When you start a new story, you will find yourself on a mostly blank screen devoid of the normal tool bars and textboxes you might be accustomed to from using other word processors or content management systems. As you start typing, a plus sign icon fades in when you move to a new line.

This icon animates in and out like this as you move through your document, being triggered into view by your actions to subtly offer options and assistance. Clicking that icon reveals a list of content types

Same Animated Menu, Different Personality

Medium isn't alone in the way it uses an animated contextual menu to help users while they're creating their post or document. Tumblr and Dropbox's Paper both also employ a similar menu. While all three of these sites have animated content-adding menus, all three animate them in slightly different ways. It's interesting to see the similarities and differences across all three sites. Each conveys a different brand and different point of view in their animation design choices.

Dropbox Paper's use of animation for this menu is the most energetic and the most pronounced. (You can see a video of it in action here: https://vimeo.com/162721550.) The animation of Paper's menu has an elastic scaling animation that has each icon bounce slightly as the list animates into view. That same lightly ecstatic bounce is seen in the motion for the main menus in Paper as well. The resulting animation reads as energetic with a touch of playfulness.

Tumblr's menu uses slightly less pronounced animation and also varies the easing used on the elements of the menu. (You can see a video of it in action here: https://vimeo.com/162721548.) The plus icon animates in with slightly elastic easing as it scales up into view. It overshoots its end size by just a little bit and snaps happily to its final size. The spin from the "+" to the "x" also uses elastic easing to overshoot the rotation a little. This makes it seem like the icon menu slides out from the rotating icon. When the menu is dismissed, all the icons fade out together and slide to the left, as if they're sliding back into the parent icon.

The elastic easing and the overshoots make Tumblr's menu feel energetic like Paper's, but since it's only used on one part of the menu, it has a more subtle

that can be inserted into your story. These additional icons also animate into view, fluidly expanding out of the first icon as they fade in.

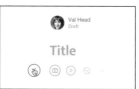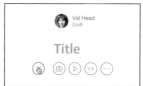

FIGURE 6.4

Medium's contextual content adding menu animates in as you move to a new section of your story and animates a series of child icons into view when you click it. See the video version here: **https://vimeo.com/162721531**.

effect. I also found it interesting to note how I projected that elastic motion onto the menu icons that weren't actually using it when using the menu. The kinetic energy from the overshoots seemed to push the child icons out into view. It wasn't until I played it back in slow motion that I realized that was just how my brain was interpreting the motion and not actually what was happening on-screen. Discovering these sleights of hand in animation is always interesting to me.

Medium's animation of this menu is the most stable and measured feeling of the three (https://vimeo.com/162721531). There are no overshoots or bouncing to be found. Each motion of the menu is eased into position with measured energy as if each icon knows exactly where it's going and confidently moves there without an overflow of energy or outside forces acting upon it. This makes them feel like the most calm or serious of the three.

When the menu opens, the "+" spins into an "x" by decidedly easing out of its motion and settling into place. The child icons scale up and fade into place with a slight offset (each one starts its entrance a fraction of a second after the one before it), which softens the effect.

One other interesting thing to note about Medium's menu animation is that all the child icons fade out as a group when dismissed with no scaling on the way out. Their exit animation is simplified compared to their entrance.

Comparing and deconstructing similar animations used by different brands is a useful exercise for helping you see how small differences in the design of animations can have a noticeable impact on the message they send. It's also a very helpful experience to have in your back pocket when you want to create a specific mood or feeling with motion in a project.

Cue the Onboarding Process with Animation

Cueing possible tasks with animation can be very effective in onboarding new users as well. When someone is completely new to your app, they could likely use a little help discovering how to use your app's interface and finding what features are available to them at any given time.

Slack uses small animated beacons to call attention to menus and features that a new user may not have discovered yet (see Figure 6.5). A subtle pulsing icon appears around one menu at a time and clicking on the icon reveals details about how that feature can be used. After you've interacted with one of these beacons, it disappears and then the next one is revealed. This continues until all the features have been explored.

The subtle pulsing beacon animation Slack uses to call attention to a so far unused featured is low-key enough that it can be ignored. New users who don't have time to explore features aren't forced into interacting with the tips before they can do anything else or forced to go through them all at once. Slack lets the onboarding process happen at whatever pace the user chooses.

FIGURE 6.5
Slack's onboarding beacons subtly notify new users of features they haven't tried yet. See the video version here: **https://vimeo. com/162721537.**

Preview the Effect of an Action

Earlier in this chapter, I mentioned that the need to show cause and effect most often comes up for more complex interactions. One of those complex interactions includes reordering content, which comes up a lot in apps or sites that include list managing or file managing actions. These aren't the only cases where animation can be useful to preview the results of an action, but they are the most readily available, so you'll notice a bit of a theme running through the next few examples.

Google Keep (**keep.google.com**) is one such app: it lets you keep track of notes, to-do lists, and reminders in a robust browser-based interface (see Figure 6.6). Google Keep uses animations to help you preview the results of your actions before you fully commit to taking them. When you start dragging one of the notes in Keep to reorder your collection, all of your notes move to make space for the note you're dragging—each one animating to what would be its new position should you choose to drop your note there. These repositioning animations give you an immediate preview of what the new order will look like in real time before you have to commit to it. A similar reordering animation occurs to show you a preview of what will happen when you delete a note before you fully commit to removing it from your collection.

Google Docs offers even more animated feedback for the more complex drag-and-drop task of reorganizing your files (see Figure 6.7). Short animations along the way keep you informed of the potential results of actions you are about to take. You see the documents you're sorting move into a neat pile under your cursor when you start the drag action. A number marker animates into view to remind you how many documents you're moving, and your full list of possible folders to drop the documents into animates open on the left side of the screen (not shown in the video version). Then when you drop the documents onto a folder, they zoom backward into the folder one at time to reinforce the fact that they've all been added to the folder as desired.

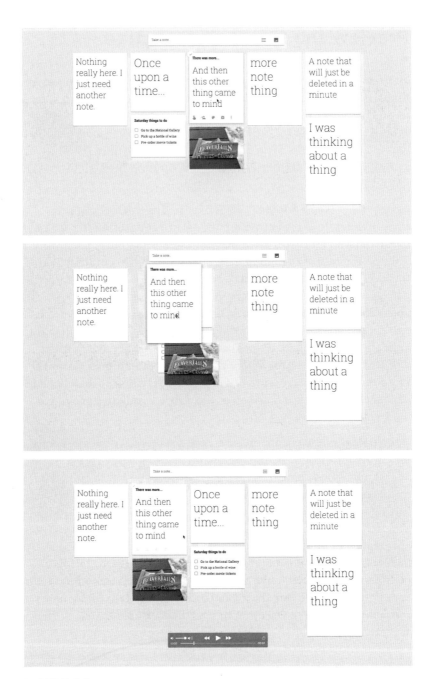

FIGURE 6.6

In Google Keep, the notes animate to new positions as you drag a note to reorder the view to show you the potential results of your action. See the video version here: **https://vimeo.com/162721546.**

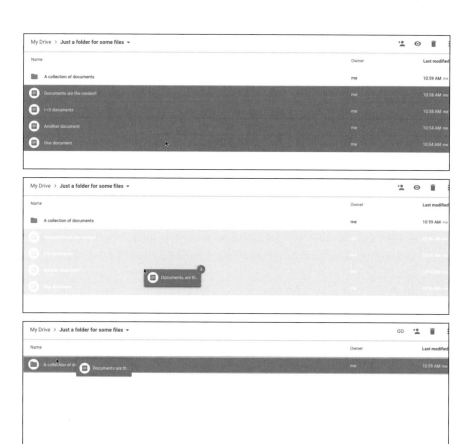

FIGURE 6.7

Google Docs uses animation to indicate how many files you're moving and where you can drop them while you are completing the action. See the video version here: **https://vimeo.com/162721545**.

The drop part of that action works in much the same way as this Codrops demo if you're interested in what the code behind interactions like this might look like.[2] Each allowable destination for the item being dragged scales up when you hover the dragged item to indicate a drop could be made there.

---

2   Codrops drag-and-drop demo: http://rfld.me/23IkY6j.

Handle Errors with Cause-and-Effect Animations

All three examples (Google Keep, Google Docs, and the Codrops demo) use animation to call out the correct places to drop dragged items. If you happened to drop a dragged item in a place it was not allowed, the dragged item(s) would animate back into its original position to show you that no action had taken place. This works well because there are very few "incorrect" places to drop the draggable items. But this might not always be the case for every drag-and-drop interaction.

In the TeuxDeux to-do app, you can drag a task anywhere on the screen, but the app only allows tasks to be dropped in certain places (see Figure 6.8).[3] You can drag a task wherever you'd like on-screen, but tasks can only be added on the next available line of any given day. In effect, that means for any given task that is being dragged, there are more "wrong" places to drop it than "right" places to drop it.

If you dropped a task in the "wrong" position, TeuxDeux could undo your action and present you with an error message telling you that you'd dragged an item into a place it can't go yet. But that would be disruptive and frustrating. Instead, TeuxDeux uses animation to suggest where the dragged task should be dropped. Then, if you happen to drop a task somewhere other than the next open line, TeuxDeux animates the dropped task from where you dropped it to the allowed position. Then the app corrects the task's position instead of going into an error state.

Animating this position change prevents any hard cuts to a reordered list or error messages telling you that you made a mistake. By showing you how it corrected the task's position, TeuxDeux both confirms that the reordering has taken place and makes it easy to see where the task now lives. That's a much more forgiving and informative solution. As the user, you can keep reordering your tasks without interruption and without any confusion as to where the task you dropped has gone.

---

3 TeuxDeux: https://teuxdeux.com/.

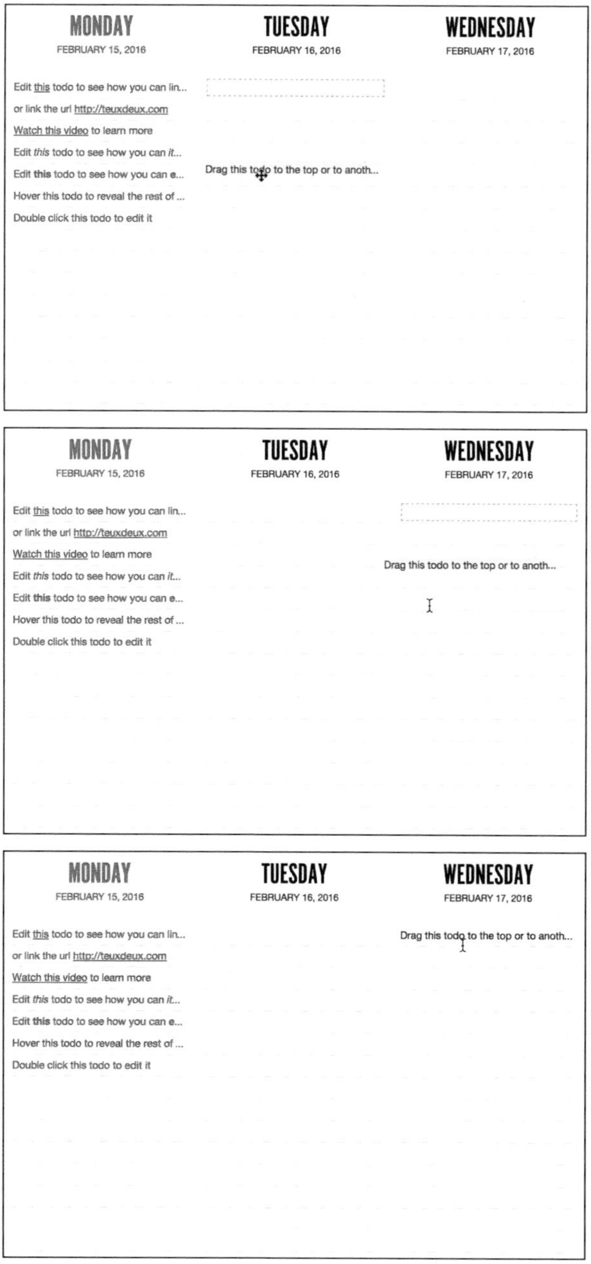

FIGURE 6.8
TeuxDeux uses animation to subtly correct you when you drop a task outside of the allowable area. You can see it in action in this video: **https://vimeo.com/162721547**.

Confirm an Action's Effect

Animation can be used to show the immediate effect of an action, which also serves to confirm the results of that action. By confirming the change visually, often by showing objects moving out of view or into a different position, your interface plainly shows the user what has happened. The result the interface shows may or may not have been the same result your user had in mind, but in either case, by explicitly showing what has changed, your user can feel more informed about what has happened.

Wunderlist, a browser-based project-planning app, does this well when it confirms that a particular item on the list has been marked as a priority item (see Figure 6.9).[4] When you click the star icon on a list item, Wunderlist confirms the action by animating the item sliding up to the top of the list while also marking the star icon with a ribbon. The whole list reorders itself right in front of you to confirm that the item is now the one with highest priority and at the top of the list. Seeing the other item move down to make space for the priority item at the top of the list also helps you keep track of how the list has been reordered. The way they move downward as a group supports the fact that they are still all the same items and in the same order as they were before.

If the list had changed, reloaded, or reordered itself without any motion instead of animating the results, you would have to take the time to reorient yourself to the list and figure out which items had changed position and where they had moved. Those two simple motions—moving the starred item to the top and the rest sliding down—save all of those questions and make the effect of the prioritizing action clear.

Space-making animations like these that show where room is being made for new content or content is being rearranged are immensely effective for keeping users informed of the results the action has taken. The animation itself doesn't have to be too showy; it just has to be enough to indicate that the other elements are moving out of the way to make space.

---

4 Wunderlist: wunderlist.com.

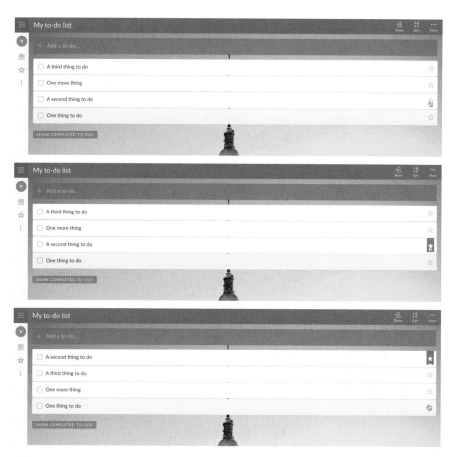

FIGURE 6.9

Wunderlist confirms a change in task priority by animating the newly prioritized items to the top of the list. You can see it in action in this video: **https://vimeo.com/162721551**.

In Campaign Monitor's email editing tool, this is done both subtly and effectively when new content blocks are added to the email layout (see Figure 6.10). As you drag a content item from the menu to the spot in the email where you'd like it to be, the space is highlighted and then the content you added grows out from that thin line of space to its full height, pushing the existing content before and after it out of the way.

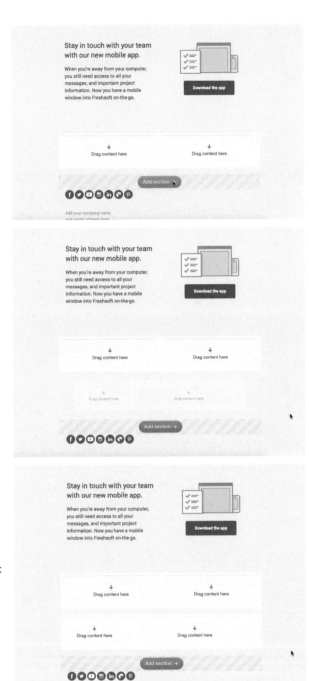

FIGURE 6.10
Campaign Monitor's email editor tool moves existing content out of the way as your newly placed content scales up to make space for itself. You can see a video of this in action here: **https://vimeo.com/162721555**.

This transition confirms where the content was dropped and high-lights which section of content is new. That may be something that the user already knows if they're paying close attention, but visually confirming it with motion provides confidence that the app is doing what was intended.

On the more complex side, Clear offers a whole collection of informa-tive animations to confirm the action of crossing an item off your to-do list (see Figure 6.11). When you mark an item as done, the back-ground color of the item first transitions to green to indicate success, and then it fades to a partially transparent gray state and moves to the bottom of the list. This animation celebrates the event of complet-ing a task on your list and visually confirms that the item was in fact marked as completed. A second click on the completed task triggers an animated exit of all the completed tasks from your list. By seeing them fall down to the bottom of the screen and out of view, it's clear that the second click action has deleted the items for you.

FIGURE 6.11
Clear uses a number of animations in sequence to celebrate complet-ing a task and marking it as done. You can see the video version here: https://vimeo.com/162721553.

Clear's more complex use of animation to confirm an action fits with its overall heavy reliance on motion as part of its design. Using animation to confirm the effect of an action can be understated, very noticeable, or somewhere in between. The deciding factor of how much animation to use to confirm a task should be how well it fits in with the overall design of the project.

When using animation to show the cause and effect of your users' actions, timing and perceived performance are critical. This type of feedback is only useful when it's immediate and when the animated action is smooth. Choppy or delayed animation will break the connection between the action and the causality it is meant to demonstrate. When that happens, the animation is more likely to confuse people rather than help them.

To be sure that your animations are demonstrating cause and effect well, prototype often and iterate on the animations and interactions until you've reached a combination that feels pleasurable to use and fits well with the other interactions in your app or site.

Staying on Point

You can use animation to show users what effect their actions have caused while they're completing a task by:

- Hinting at affordances with animation.
- Cueing the next step in a series of tasks with animation.
- Previewing of the effect an action will have before it is taken.
- Confirming an action's effect once it has been taken.

CHAPTER 7

Using Animation for Feedback

Giving good feedback is imperative for good interface design. When something is happening behind the scenes—whether it's fetching data or completing a request—it's important to show that something *is* happening, or *has* happened, even if the feedback is that something went wrong along the way. Without feedback, users are left to wonder if their request was acted upon or heard at all. Good feedback keeps the conversation between the interface and user going during those unavoidable waiting periods.

The attention grabbing power of animation is one of the reasons that animation can be so useful for giving feedback. But that's not the only characteristic of animation that lends itself well to giving feedback. The time-based nature of animation is also helpful for giving feedback in a useful and meaningful way.

Incorporating animation into the feedback mechanisms you design can help make them more timely and effective. In this chapter, you'll see some examples of how animation can be used to improve feedback in forms, loaders, multifunctional elements, and perceived performance. There are lots of opportunities for animation to help step up your feedback game.

Animate Effective Error Messages

No one likes getting error messages, and an error message that's too easy to miss is even more frustrating. The whole interaction around error messages can be stressful—both for the people who receive them and the people designing them. Using animation in the design of error messages can help make them stand out more easily, while also taking advantage of the dimension of time.

Stripe Checkout uses animation well in its error messages (see Figure 7.1). On larger screens, the whole form shakes with a brisk shaking motion upon attempting to submit the form when errors are present. This creates feedback that is very difficult to miss, and it also gives a nod to a common real-world motion of someone shaking his or her head "no." It's almost like the form is shaking its head at you.[1]

---

1 Improve the Payment Experience with Animations: http://rfld.me/1qVnubl.

FIGURE 7.1

Stripe Checkout's form animates to shake its head at you to indicate that one of the fields has an error. See the error animation in action in this video: **https://vimeo.com/162722757**.

In Stripe Checkout, the shaking animation is paired with a red outline around the problematic fields to indicate where the error is. Animation is used as the primary indicator of an error, and the outline is the secondary indicator. Checkout continues to use animation to indicate form errors even on smaller screens, although it changes its approach slightly for the smaller space.

On smaller screens, red animated arrows appear in the fields that contain errors. The arrows shake back and forth in a similar manner to how the whole form moved on larger screens, and the arrows are outlined in red. In both contexts, a shaking animation and the red outline are used to indicate errors on the form. Using motion to indicate the errors, instead of introducing an error message that will cause the page layout to reflow, means that all the form fields are in the same place as when it was being filled out. Users won't have to rescan the page, or the form, to find their place again.

You probably noticed that one of the other strengths of animation is at play in this example as well. The shaking animation contrasts with all the other animations in Checkout, which helps it stand out in the design even more and demand your attention.

For a slightly different approach to animating error message feedback, **Crowdcast.io** also uses animation for its error messages (see Figure 7.2). The motion used to present the error messages helps differentiate it from the orange focus outline used elsewhere in their form. Animating this feedback allows them to use the same space for different error messages while calling attention to the feedback by putting it in motion.

FIGURE 7.2
Crowdcast.io's animated error messages. You can see them in action here: https://vimeo.com/162722758.

Visually Confirm Tasks Without Losing Your Place

Animating feedback can open up opportunities to provide feedback on interactions as they are happening without disrupting the entire interface visually. Small changes of state—even just within something like a button—can give added feedback on what is happening behind the scenes.

The Slides.com interface takes advantage of this in a number of places throughout its web-based interface. Their buttons often double as processing indicators or confirmation messages, one of which is the log-in button that turns into a loading indicator as you're being logged in (see Figure 7.3). This helps to show that something is happening and that your button click has registered as loaders are meant to do—all with the elements that are already present on-screen.

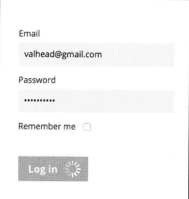

FIGURE 7.3

Slides' log-in button animates to act as both the log-in button and the account loading indicator. You can see it in action on **Slides.com**, or in this video: **https://vimeo.com/162723544**.

Within the application itself, while you're creating a presentation, you encounter similar kinds of animated feedback. The save button icon animates from a disk icon, to a loading spinner, to a check mark (see Figure 7.4). It indicates along the way that your data is in the process of being saved, and then confirms that it has been saved—all within the very compact space of the button you've clicked. The animations allow this button to have both multiple states and multiple functionalities.

Other buttons in the interface have multiple functionalities as well. That's part of why these are so effective for **Slides.com**. The consistency with which they've chosen to give their animated feedback—in this case, through multifunctional buttons—makes it easier to know where to look for this feedback. As you use the interface more and more, you start picking up on these consistencies, which makes the behaviors of the app feel consistent and familiar to you over time.

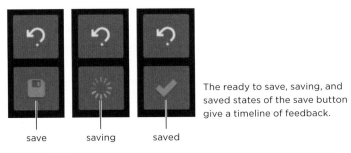

The ready to save, saving, and saved states of the save button give a timeline of feedback.

save   saving   saved

FIGURE 7.4
By transitioning between these three states, the save button in Slides gives timely feedback as to the status of the current document and what is going on behind the scenes. See it in action in the video version: **https://vimeo.com/162723547**.

Stripe Checkout provides similar feedback through its Pay button (see Figure 7.5). The Pay button animates from its initial state, to a loader, to a confirmation checkmark in order to indicate that the payment has been processed. This same behavior happens on both the larger viewport version and the smaller viewport version of the payment form for a consistent experience.

FIGURE 7.5
Stripe Checkout's pay (or donate) button does triple duty as the button, loading indicator, and payment confirmation all in one place. See it in action in this video clip: **https://vimeo.com/162723550**.

Loader Animations That Convey Progress

Loading animations is a common way to show users that something is going on in the background—that the machines behind the interface are working on something, and they're not ready to show it just yet. These loaders are often animated, and are usually generic or nonspecific about the activity taking place—for example, showing a spinner or counting up to 100%. There's an opportunity here to do something better for your audience. The more informative and customized your loader animations are, the more likely they are to create a positive experience for your audience. The more real feedback you can give, the more satisfactory the loading experience will be for all involved.

For example, Shopify.com has a very informative loader that appears when you set up a new account (see Figure 7.6). The loader animation consists of a few lines of text fading in and out as your new account is created in the background. Each line suggests a step that is taking place behind the scenes: "1 of 4: Creating your account" "2 of 4: Initializing your store." These exact steps may not really be taking place as each line appears, and the loader may not truly represent how long it takes to create a new account, but neither of those things matter. What matters is that people waiting for this loader to do its thing feel informed and confident that what they have requested is happening. Plus, it makes for a much more pleasant waiting period— one that fosters a sense of anticipation instead of frustration or stress. The way the information is offered step-by-step, focusing on the progress, makes it seem as if the waiting time is shorter, which is an added bonus.

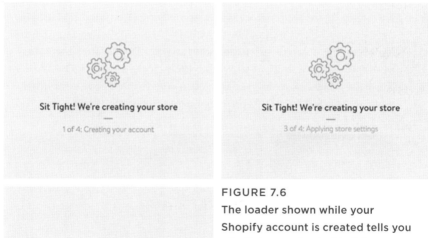

Sit Tight! We're creating your store

1 of 4: Creating your account

Sit Tight! We're creating your store

3 of 4: Applying store settings

Success! Your store is ready to go

4 of 4: Applying default theme

FIGURE 7.6
The loader shown while your Shopify account is created tells you what's happening behind the scenes as you wait. Watch the full loading process in this video: **https://vimeo.com/162722759**.

Contextually Fit Loader Animations, Not Generic Spinners

Realistically, there are going to be times when you really don't know how long a loading operation will take while things are happening in the background. Sometimes, it really is a sit-back-and-wait kind of situation, and there is no additional or incremental feedback available to share. In those cases, creating a custom loading animation, instead of opting for a generic loading bar or spinner, can improve the experience.

A customized loader can create added trust because it's not the same generic spinner that has let you down a million times before. Anecdotally, as users of an interface, we're willing to give a customer loader—one that's new to us—the benefit of the doubt. If nothing else, a customized contextually appropriate loader animation will show a greater attention to detail and care put into the design of the experience.

The Sure Payroll and FreeAgent loaders don't give any indication as to exactly what is happening behind the scenes or how far the task you're waiting for has progressed, but they do provide an interesting and visually fitting indication that something is happening (see Figures 7.7 and 7.8). The calculator animation appears when Sure Payroll is processing a newly submitted payroll, and FreeAgent shows the numbers jumping into a box while you export your user data. Both of these are much more enjoyable to encounter than a generic spinner, even if they don't actually provide more information than one.

FIGURE 7.7

Sure Payroll's loader animates sums on a calculator while it calculates your total payroll costs. Watch the video here to see it in action: **https://vimeo.com/162723551.**

FIGURE 7.8

FreeAgent's custom designed loader shows numbers jumping into a box as you wait for your user data to be exported. Watch the video version here: **https://vimeo.com/163024305.**

In my years of designing websites, I've always felt that custom loaders made for a more satisfactory experience, but it was never something I looked into beyond that gut feeling. The folks at Viget, on the other hand, have done a small study on loaders and came to some interesting conclusions.[2] Their small experiment found that participants were more willing to wait for custom loading animations than generic loading animations. And participants were even more willing to wait for loaders with novel and engaging animations. Those are some interesting results! There are many other contextual aspects—especially user context—at play for any given loading situation than could be accounted for in this experiment. But overall, this experiment supports the idea that investing a little time into creating a customized and interesting loading animation will pay off with positive benefits to the user experience.

Another recent piece on loading animations confirms that the topic of loading animations is often more nuanced than you might initially think. In the article "The Psychology of Waiting, Loading Animations, and Facebook,"[3] Rusty Mitchell suggests, based on findings from Facebook's research, that when load times are very long, generic spinners cause users to blame their device for the slowness, not the app that is being slow. While very intriguing, that finding brings up more questions than it answers with so few details available about the actual study it stems from. The main thing it suggests is that there is a limit as to how long users will wait, regardless of how informative or well designed the loader animation is.

2 Experiments in Loading—How Long Will You Wait? http://rfld.me/23II51I.

3 The Psychology of Waiting, Loading Animations, and Facebook: http://rfld.me/1VnY42y.

Make Waiting Go by Faster

One of the often overlooked benefits of animation's use of time is that you can use it to make waiting times seem to go by more quickly (see Figure 7.9). An animation can't exist without taking up time, since time is part of its very definition. When you take animation and use it where you essentially have time to kill, it can have positive results. Filling up time that would be there anyway with an informative animation can make that time seem to go by faster, thereby improving the perceived performance of load times and other unavoidable waits.

FIGURE 7.9
Facebook uses animated lines and squares arranged in a way that suggests the content is arriving soon so that load times will be perceived as happening faster.

Instances where additional information needs to be fetched from the server, data requires processing, or similar behind-the-scenes activity needs to occur are perfect opportunities to use animation to fill that time in a meaningful and useful way.

Showing skeleton content while content is being loaded can make it seem like things are loading faster. A study from the VTT Technical Research Centre of Finland[4] found that showing a hint of content was perceived as faster by users when compared with a loading

---

4 Animated UI Transitions and Perceptions of Time—a User Study on Animated Effects on a Mobile Screen by Huhtala, Sarjaoja, Mäntyjärvi, Insomursu and Häkkilä. Published in *Proceedings of the SIGCHI Conference on Human Factors in Computing Systems*: http://rfld.me/263HjgO.

spinner animation. The main findings of the study indicate that the sooner you show some hint of the new content, the faster the load time is perceived to be. Findings like these are likely why we're seeing skeleton content used more and more instead of generic loaders, or in conjunction with loaders, in many sites and applications. Luke Wroblewski came to similar conclusions based on his work on the Polar app, suggesting "Skeleton screens are another way to focus on progress instead of wait times."[5]

Both the research on loading animations and the potential perceived performance gains are very convincing evidence to consider designing a more creative loader solution when wait times must occur. A more creative solution that hints at the content to come, could mean the wait times are perceived as taking less time by focusing on the progress being made.

Whether the behind-the-scenes progress is known or unknown, loading time gives you an opportunity to show that you care about your users when you design the animation well. Designing the details in these situations can go far toward earning your users' trust and patience. The same applies to all the feedback examples discussed in this chapter. These points of potential mistakes, errors, or waiting are chances to shine with your attention to detail and transparency.

Staying on Point

Animation can help make feedback better by:

- Animating effective and attention-grabbing error messages.
- Visually confirming behind-the-scenes tasks in context.
- Animating meaningful loading indicators.
- Providing an early hint of content to make wait times feel shorter.

---

5 Mobile Design Details: Avoid the Spinner: http://rfld.me/24tBOGu.

Using Animation to Demonstrate

If a picture is worth a thousand words, then an animation is worth a billion. The numbers aren't real, but the sentiment is true. A lot of information can be conveyed in a short amount of time with animation. Its ability to communicate includes being able to be interpreted quickly due to its time-based nature and to create an emotional statement with its movement and gestures. A lot of information can be packaged up into just a second or two! You can use this to your advantage when demonstrating how a product or service works or by telling the story behind a product.

Demonstrate Functionality

Using animation, you can exhibit exactly what a specific feature of a product does more efficiently than you can in writing. You can show exactly how something works visually and have it understood immediately. (Of course, it's still best to also offer a written equivalent for those who can't see your animation or prefer that method.)

MailChimp takes advantage of this by opting for a short and informative animation on its home page instead of a carousel or static hero image. When their home page loads, a short (less than 2 seconds) animation starts, as shown in Figure 8.1. It shows various types of content blocks being dragged from a panel on the right to an email on the left. When the content is dropped, it's added to the email content. This gives a succinct overview of how MailChimp's email building editor works.

The animation is focused. It doesn't show everything the email editor can do. Nor does it show every single thing that MailChimp's products and services can do. It knows what it wants to say, and it gets to the point. This is a big part of why it works so well. There are no superfluous movements or effects.

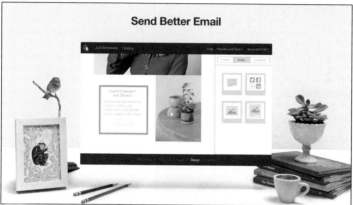

FIGURE 8.1

MailChimp uses a short 3-second animation on its home page to demonstrate key features of its product instead of a hero image or carousel. You can see the animation in action in this video: **https://vimeo.com/162724775**.

Demonstrate with Animations in the Onboarding Process

Short demonstrational animations are also common in the onboarding process. (The process[es] you use to orient new users to the features of your app or site.) Onboarding new users is a critical task, especially for apps that may be new to the market or contain somewhat complex interactions. Animation can be a huge help when attention spans are short and the information being conveyed is critical to using the app successfully.

Apple uses animation in its onboarding sequence of OSX updates to demonstrate the new additions and features (see Figure 8.2). As you cycle through the introductory screens after installing the latest OS, certain tasks are animated to demonstrate how they work, or to identify where certain triggers are located on the screen.

FIGURE 8.2

Apple uses demonstration animations in its OS onboarding process to demonstrate how new features behave. You can see it in action in this video: **https://vimeo.com/162724777**.

Often, animation is used in this way to demonstrate gestures or application-specific interactions, giving new users some insider information on how to get the most out of the app they've just signed up for. Demonstrating app-specific interactions by showing them in an animated way not only helps make them easier to discover, it can also make them feel more familiar when it comes time to use them.

Hootsuite does this in its onboarding sequence as well. Hootsuite steps its viewers through the three most important tasks that can be accomplished with its app the first time they open it (see Figure 8.3). The tasks are shown in the same sequence they would be completed by someone using the service, and each task's screen shows an animated demonstration of how that feature works.

FIGURE 8.3

Hootsuite's onboarding animations demonstrates how the app works before users start using it. You can see Hootsuite's onboarding in action in this video: https://vimeo.com/162724780.

Onboarding animations can go beyond just being factual or literal in their demonstration of features. Fun or conceptual animation can be effective in onboarding as well. Dropbox uses conceptual animations to show files flying through the air behind planes or popping up in a forest (see Figure 8.4). These animations show what Dropbox does in a way that's a bit whimsical—focusing on showing what you can do with the app in a way that's much more compelling and injected with personality through animation.

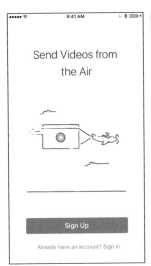

FIGURE 8.4
Dropbox's onboarding animations have a little fun showing you all the places your files can now go with you. See the video version here: https://vimeo.com/162724786.

Show Personality and Purpose

For some sites, the bulk of their content is a conceptual message more so than text and images. This is especially true for a site whose purpose is to be a cover page for a downloadable app. The main point of such a site is to encourage people to download the app and to make the app seem desirable to its intended audience. Doing this conceptually is faster than spelling out every single feature in words. This approach aims to make a more emotional connection with the potential audience. In some cases, when the product is still in development, spelling out specific features may not be an option at all. These sites use animation, concept, and imagery to get their core values across and tell a story that will hopefully appeal to their core audience.

The initial Marked.io site is a good example of this idea, despite the fact that the site is no longer live (see Figure 8.5). There is very little in the way of traditional content on this page. There is the app's name, a tagline, a short one-sentence description, and a short sign-up form to collect email addresses if you're intrigued enough to want to know more.

Marked — Save. Share. Discover.

Simple, clever bookmarking. Opening to limited beta very soon, if you would like to take part please register below or read the FAQs.

Email address [Send]

FIGURE 8.5
Marked.io's build-in animation tells the story of the application and what it does on a conceptual level. You can see the archived version in this video: **https://vimeo .com/162724788.**

The bulk of the way this page communicates is with the build-in animation that shows a man on an expedition marking his place at a summit with a flag. The view zooms out to reveal the short bit of text content for the site. The animation takes less than 2 seconds, but it conveys exactly what the app is for—marking your place—and does it in a way that attempts to differentiate it from every other bookmarking app out there by telling their story in a unique way. The style of the illustrations and animation says more about the app than the short amount of text on the page.

Piction (pictionapp.com), an iOS app for adding captions to photos, uses a conceptual build-in animation on its site for a similar purpose (see Figure 8.6). A different photo fades in to fill the background each time you load the page; then the content and main call to action fade in to view as well. The main visual element is an iPhone, which plays a short demonstration animation of how the app works after it fades into view.

More information is conveyed with the animations—both the build-in and the demonstration—than any of the written content on the page. The fade-ins of the content's entrances create a dreamlike feel, especially when combined with the soft focus of the background images. The animation they've used—even in such small amounts—works to create that concept and make an emotional connection with the viewers along with the rest of the design choices.

These build-in animations are a little reminiscent of the Flash intros of the past. They aim to say something about the company or product like intros did, and they're animated like intros were, but that's where the similarities end. Build-in opening animations are shorter and less obtrusive than the Flash intros of the past were. They're natively part of the site, not a separate thing that has been tacked on the front of them. The fact that they use native browser technology allows them to be nonblocking; they don't force users to wait before they can interact with any of the site elements. Perhaps the biggest difference between these and the skip-intros of the past is the clear conceptual message and focus of these builds when they're done successfully. They make a short focused point about the product instead of acting as a commercial or trying to tell the entire story from start to end.

FIGURE 8.6
Piction's site build-in gives a quick demonstration of what you can do with the app. You can see it in action in this video: **https://vimeo.com/162724791**.

Not Repeating the "Skip Intro" Era

If you're reading this book, I assume that you have no interest in re-creating the skip intro era of Flash sites that egregiously imposed auto-playing music and animation as a fancy front door to their website. Not only are such things out of style now but they wouldn't be effective on today's web. You could probably argue they were never effective, but that's a different story. As an industry, we know better now anyway.

There was nothing wrong with the desire to use emotional design and say something about the personality of the product with motion. The problem was the method: holding your audience hostage with your intro and forcing them to download third-party players to watch it. That part wasn't cool. There are plenty of other and better choices now.

With the current state of web animation—and the continuous way the technology is improving—there are better tools available to design for emotion and convey the personality of a company or product with motion.

If you're ever worried about it, to be really sure you're not repeating intro problems of the past, here are some things to check:

- Make sure that any build animations are less than 5 seconds long (longer and Web Content Accessibility Guidelines [WCAG] recommends play/pause controls, so staying well under that is a safe area to aim for).

- Focus on having one clear short message or concept that the animation is conveying.

- Have the end state of the build-in animation be usable items of the interface.

- Avoid introducing extra elements just for show. Make the "intro" a part of the interface as much as possible.

- If the motion is large or drastic, consider giving users an option to reduce it or turn it off. (More on that in Chapter 12, "Animating Responsibly.")

Animate Conceptual Illustrations

Animations can be conceptual and editorial in much the same way that illustrations can be. When they're used in this way, they work to demonstrate a high-level concept or part of the story. Using animation for this purpose lends itself well to long-form articles and stories.

The glitch concept for the "Anatomy of a Hack" article on *The Verge* starts in the header video and then continues with the subtle glitch animation in the article's headings (see Figure 8.7).[1] The glitch

FIGURE 8.7

The "Anatomy of a Hack" article uses glitch animations in the header image and headlines to boost the editorial concept throughout the article. You can see a video of it in action here: **https://vimeo.com/162724787**.

---

1 Anatomy of a Hack, The Verge: **http://rfld.me/1V4mQ8b**.

animation of the headings carries the glitch concept throughout the entire article. The flowchart that diagrams the path of the hack also animates as you scroll through the article, highlighting the part of the path you're currently reading about. Both sets of animations help pull you into the story, as well as keep you on track of where you are in the story.

In the "Sound Decisions" article, even more abstract editorial animations are used throughout to create a visual representation of the sounds that are discussed.[2] These animations are more illustrative than the previous article; they're not interactive at all (see Figure 8.8). But the personality and motion used in each one perfectly evokes the same qualities of the sounds being discussed. A static illustration could not have the same impact on readers.

Both of these articles use animation successfully to help convey a specific concept and message. All the animations used reinforce either the design concept or the content of the story; they're not just there for show or decoration. The fact that everything—including the animation—is focused on furthering the story is what makes these editorial animations work so well.

FIGURE 8.8
The "Sound Decisions" article uses animation to demonstrate and embody the sounds it describes throughout the article. You can see a video of it in action here: **https://vimeo.com/162724792.**

---

2 Sound Decisions, The Verge: **http://rfld.me/1WuaoOs.**

Staying on Point

- Focus: Each animation should have a clear focus of either a single feature or a single aspect of the story to tell.

- Short length: Keep the animation on point and show a single task or action at a time.

- Don't block access to content or navigation.

CHAPTER 9

Using Animation to Express Your Brand

Each animation in an interface tells a micro story, and as a user encounters more and more animations throughout your site or product, these micro stories add up to reveal the personality and story of the brand or product behind them. The animations create an impression; they give your brand a certain personality. It's up to us as designers to take control of the combined story that animations are telling about the brand we're working on. Your animations will be much more effective if you intentionally design the additional messages they're sending.

Brand animation design guidelines aren't something entirely new, of course. Brands have been expressing themselves in motion in commercials, TV bumpers, video titles, and similar places for years, and they've had guidelines for those mediums. What's new is the idea of needing animation design guidelines for the web or interfaces. Even if your brand will never be in a traditional commercial or video, having a website is enough of a reason to need a motion style guide these days.

How Your Brand Moves Tells Its Story

Deciding what you use animation for, and how you implement it, for a particular project defines how you express your brand or tell your brand's story with animation. Often, the decisions of which properties to animate or what easing to use on which elements is done at the component or page level without considering the bigger picture. Assembling a global set of rules about motion and animation for your entire project will help you make more cohesive animation decisions moving forward. These choices lead to more consistent design decisions surrounding animation and make your design stronger overall. It requires you to go back and forth between the big picture of the overall project and the more detailed components, but your entire design will benefit from looking at the project from both perspectives as you work.

There are two approaches to begin defining how your brand expresses itself in motion. The first is to go from the bottom up: start by evaluating what you already have and build from there. The second is to go from the top down: first, determine what it is your brand should be saying about itself on a high level, and then determine how individual animations will express that concept.

The first approach works best for existing projects that already use animation. There could be hidden gems of communication to build upon in the animations you've already designed—ones that will inform the bigger picture you're working to define. The second approach is generally your only option when starting a brand new project, as there won't be any existing animation to start from. Whichever approach you choose (or even if you use both), you'll arrive at the same end result, a common set of guidelines for putting your brand in motion, so they are equally good places to begin.

Defining Your Brand in Motion from the Bottom Up

Before you start documenting for the future, you need to get a good picture of what you're currently using animation for. It's hard to move forward before knowing where you currently stand. (That is, unless you're planning to throw it all out and start over.) For existing projects that already use animation, you can start with a motion audit to find all the instances and ways you're currently using animation. Collecting these in one place will identify the common threads and even help you eliminate unnecessary duplicated or overly similar animations. A motion audit will focus your animation efforts and the design reasoning behind them.

TIP MOTION AUDITS

A motion audit gathers up all the interface animations you're currently using to identify patterns and evaluate their effectiveness as a group.

The Motion Audit

To collect all your animations in one place, you'll need some screen recording software that will output video. QuickTime is a handy built-in option for Macs, but a more specialized tool like ScreenFlow can save you some time with its more robust cropping and editing tools. Use whichever tool is easiest and fastest for you. The exact software used is less important than the end collection and what it will tell you.

How to do a motion audit (see Figure 9.1):

- Collect screen recordings of every animation currently on your site. (Be sure to get a recording of all the different states for interactive animations.)

- Crop and edit the video clips as needed to focus in on the animations.

- Assemble all the video clips into one document and group them in categories according to content type (for example, one slide for all the button animations, one slide for navigation animations, etc.).

- Review the document with your team to evaluate your brand's existing animation style.

When you have all of those in one place, you can look for global trends, find potential redundancies, and most importantly, evaluate if the way you're currently using animation accurately reflects the personality of your brand or product.

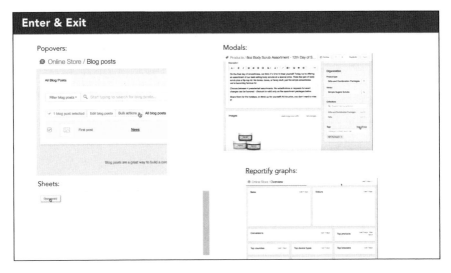

FIGURE 9.1

A screenshot of a page/slide of a motion audit document created for Shopify.

Recording Animations

For the screen recording part of motion audits, I like to use Screen-Flow (telestream.net/screenflow/). It's Mac only, but Camtasia (techsmith.com/camtasia.html) offers similar functionality for both Windows and Mac. The QuickTime player that comes installed with OSX is also an option. It's especially good for recording animations from an iPhone. Just plug it into the computer and select it as a camera in QuickTime.

The Motion Audit Document

My preferred software for the end document is Keynote. (PowerPoint would do just fine here as well.) I prefer it because it makes it easy to set each animation's video clip to play when clicked and because it lends itself well to be projected and discussed as a group.

When Keynote isn't an option, creating a web-based motion audit is a good alternative. It's easy to share, and the video clips can be played directly from within the web pages. I find that having the videos playable from the document is really useful. Often, you'll discover animations that some of your teammates weren't aware of or maybe haven't encountered in a while.

The key is having an end result that can be shared and discussed easily. So if there's another format that your team has a strong preference for, you can make that work, too.

Evaluate Your Existing Animation's Design

The first question you'll want to investigate is: Does the personality expressed by the existing animations fit your brand? Look at the qualities of the animations you're using to answer this one. What kind of personality traits do the easing and timing used convey? If it's snappy and bouncy, does that match your brand's personality and energy? If it's all stable ease-in-outs, is your brand personality also stable and decided? If you find the mood of the animations doesn't fit your brand's personality, small changes to the easing and timing could make a huge difference to bring the animation in line with your brand.

If the personality conveyed from your animations is all over the place and not cohesive at all, starting over and taking the top-down approach described might be the next best step. It's often easier to work from the top down with a clear vision, as opposed to trying to fix a huge group of existing animations that are all a little bit off.

If the personality conveyed by your animations does fit your brand perfectly, great! Take a detailed look at what all these animations have in common. List the easing, timing, and other design choices they have in common. This will be the basis of your brand's animation style guide.

Evaluate Your Existing Animation's Purpose

Next, look at the purpose of the animations you've collected. How are they aiding your users in their tasks? Are they bringing something positive to the experience? Their purpose can be anything from something tactical like providing feedback to something more branding related like expressing your brand's personality. Challenge yourself to articulate a purpose for each one to help you evaluate how useful they are. If there's no definable purpose for an animation to be there, consider eliminating or redesigning it to have a solid purpose and goal. (Good UX purposes for animation are covered in Chapters 4 through 8.)

It's also helpful to group the animations in your motion audit by their purpose—gathering up all the animations that are there to give feedback into one section, for example. This can reveal some helpful insights, similarities, and patterns among animations that share a similar purpose.

Define Your Brand in Motion from the Top Down

If your brand doesn't currently use any animation or if you're starting a new project, you can develop your brand's animation design guidelines from the top down instead. That is, start from your brand's design philosophy or the traits your brand aims to embody and decide how to translate those into animation. It's starting from a different place, but it gets you to the same end goal of having specific and defined ways that your brand will exist in motion.

The Words You Use to Describe Your Brand

Start with the adjectives that you use to describe your brand or product. The description of the personality or feelings it aims to create. Is your brand energetic? Friendly? Strong? Playful? Stable? All this descriptive language can be translated into motion just like it can for other design tools like typography and color. Animation speaks in similar ways.

A great place to look for these descriptive words is in your copywriting guidelines or voice and tone guidelines. Many of the same words used to describe how to write for your brand can be directly applied to motion as well. Brand style guides or brand books can also be a good source for descriptive language.

If none of the above exists for your brand, you'll need to do a little work to define your brand's voice. "5 Easy Steps to Define and Use Your Brand Voice" by Erika Heald[1] could be helpful for a quick start. Or to get even deeper into defining your brand, I recommend reading *Designing Brand Identity* by Alina Wheeler.[2]

Energetic

If your brand is energetic, friendly, or bold, animation that relies on a lot of overshoots or follow-through and anticipation can help convey a sense of energy. Softly overshooting the target position can make animations feel both friendly and energetic. Drastic overshoots and quick speed changes read as bold and outgoing. Taken even further, adding a bit of bounce to overshoots or follow-through can convey a sense of even more energy in a movement—so much energy that an object has to bounce off its destination once or twice before it settles (see Figure 9.2).

Quick, soft movements—like overshoots—tend to read as energetic in a friendly way. On the other hand, quick movement with sharp changes in direction can suggest impatience, curtness, or urgency. That kind of movement is difficult to show in print, but you can see a video version here (https://vimeo.com/162725654) to see what I mean.

---

1 5 Easy Steps to Define and Use Your Brand Voice by Erika Heald: http://rfld.me/1VGj9pw.

2 *Designing Brand Identity* by Alina Wheeler: http://rfld.me/24tBQhG.

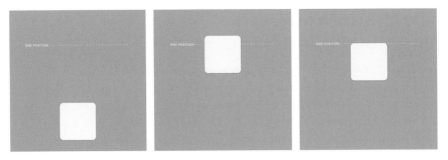

FIGURE 9.2
Follow-through and overshoots in motion come across as energetic. The more exaggerated the movement, the more energy is implied. See it in action in this video: **https://vimeo.com/162725652.**

Playful and Friendly

Playful brands can take advantage of squash and stretch to convey that playfulness (see Figure 9.3). Squash and stretch also makes movements read as energetic. However, beware, because it can also make motion look childish or sloppy if it's done with too much of a heavy hand. But, on the other hand, when it's done well, it can really set you apart.

Bouncy easing can also evoke friendliness or playfulness. Wobbly bounces can seem playful and elastic, while springy bounces can seem friendly.

FIGURE 9.3
Squash and stretch tends to create a sense of playfulness and a little goes a long way. See it in action in this video: **https://vimeo.com/162725656.**

Decisive and Sure

Ease-in-outs—that is any easing that gradually speeds up into the action, is fastest in the middle, and then slows at the end of the action—are balanced and stable. They produce animation that accelerates into the action and then slows down to hit its end target exactly and with precision and decisiveness. Sticking with variations of ease-in-outs can communicate a sense of stability and balance for your brand. A variation of ease-in-out easing applied to a simple horizontal movement would look like this video example in Figure 9.4.

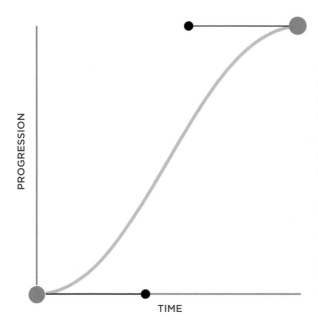

FIGURE 9.4
Motion with ease-in-out easing like the graph to the left, and similar easing curve variations, tends to read as calm and decisive action because elements move fastest in the middle of the action and decelerate into their final position. You can see the resulting motion in this video: **https://vimeo.com/162725657**.

Calm

The amount of movement you employ can also say something about your brand. Animation doesn't necessarily have to include large movements or even include motion at all. Smaller movements read as more calm and subtle than larger more drastic movements. Using smaller movements can contribute to the stable and calm personality of your brand.

You can still imply the same kinds of movements, just in a less drastic way. For example, when you aim to create small movements, you might have a modal animate into place from 50% of the way down the screen instead of 100% off-screen past the bottom of the visible area (see Figure 9.5).

SMALL MOVEMENTS

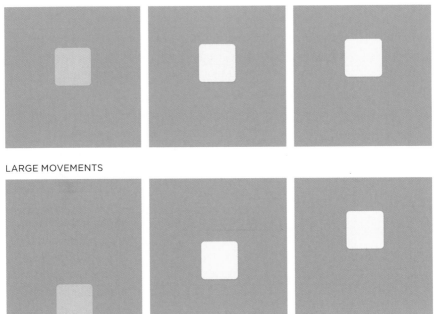

LARGE MOVEMENTS

FIGURE 9.5
Both squares in the frames above arrive at the same destination, but the first one gets there by moving a shorter distance. This smaller movement often reads as feeling calmer and more subdued than larger movements. See both in action in video: small movements (**https://vimeo.com/162725660**) vs. large movements (**https://vimeo.com/163036094**).

Stable

Animating properties like opacity and blur instead of creating movement is another way of conveying a sense of calm and stability (see Figure 9.6). (Animating these properties will change the appearance of the object—making it more transparent or blurred, for example—but because the position of the element isn't being animated, no movement will occur.) It can also convey a sense of softness or even feel dreamy, depending on how softly you use the opacity and blurs. Sticking to these nonmovement properties can still say so much about your brand in small spaces where motion may not be possible or desirable.

FIGURE 9.6

Animating nonmotion properties, like blur and opacity, can read as more stable and subtle. See it in action in this video: **https://vimeo.com/162725661**.

These are just the start of adjectives to consider when trying to convey a specific type of energy in the design of your animation. Like most other design tools, it's more of an art than a science. Experiment with the guidelines to find what expresses your brand best for you.

Referencing Motion from Real Life

Looking to the physical world can be a great option for finding your brand's style for motion by finding a physical object or creature to emulate with your on-screen animation. Technically, you could choose anything at all to base your motion on, but this works best when the thing you choose is relevant—either literally or metaphorically—to your product or brand.

IBM has done a wonderful job of this with its Machines in Motion design guidelines. IBM used to make those giant, room-sized computers, typewriters, and other hardware before becoming the IBM they are today. They decided to reach back to their rich history as a company when defining how they would express their brand in motion (see Figure 9.7).

They used these past machines to inform their motion design efforts on two levels. On a high level, they chose four machine traits that all their interface motions should embody: agility, efficiency, precision, and order. From there, they got more specific and paired motion from the actual machines with screen-based equivalent animations. On-screen menu drawers are animated to have the same motion as the carriage return motion of a 1970s IBM typewriter. Loading spinners are animated to have the same acceleration patterns as reel-to-reel tapes of an old mainframe's tape drives.

FIGURE 9.7

IBM's Machines in Motion design guidelines pair movements from the physical products IBM used to make with matching motion for their animation interactions. See **http://rfld.me/1VsjV9H**.

These one-to-one translations of motion from the historical real-world objects to the screen-based motion inform all of their motion design decisions. If you have physical objects, either historical or not, that are significant to your brand or product, you could develop your own guidelines using this same approach.

A more metaphorical approach to emulating real-world objects can work well, too. Finding a particular dance piece or animal movement that speaks to the same personality values as your brand can be a great place to start. Music can be a source of motion inspiration, even if you're not including any sound in your interface. Choosing a specific rhythm or phrasing from music to apply to your animation's movement brings a whole new dimension to the idea of UX choreography. There are so many possibilities out there. Find something that feels inspiring for your brand and explore how it can establish a cohesive thread through all your animations.

Staying on Point

- Animation design guidelines or values can help keep your brand's motion efforts consistent and cohesive.

- Collecting and evaluating existing animations as a group with a motion audit can give you valuable insight into how you're currently using animation.

- The same words you use to describe your brand and its values can be translated into motion to define your brand's motion style.

- Looking to real-world objects or animals to emulate can also help define what your brand looks like in motion.

PART III

Animation in Your Work and Process

So often, animation doesn't get much thought or attention until the very end of a project. Finally, all the hard parts of the design have been figured out, so it's finally time to think about the fun details. But by that point, it's often too late. Time-lines and budgets are pushing their limits, and advocating for your animation ideas becomes increasingly difficult against those odds.

By leaving it to the end, you're treating animation like the icing on the cake. In previous chapters, we've covered many ways that design can benefit from animation, but it can be so much more than just "icing." In order to get those benefits, however, animation has to be part of the whole cake, not just the icing—it needs to be a part of your entire process all along the way.

This last part of the book focuses on how to find a place for animation in your current design process, and how to make the most efficient and useful prototypes along the way.

Where Animation Fits in Your Design Process

Exactly where and how animation best fits into your design process will depend on your team dynamics. No two teams work exactly the same way or use the same process. This chapter includes a number of suggestions on where and how to fit the discussion of animation into your process. You might decide to implement a few or all of these suggestions, but the most important part is getting animation into your process in a way that plays to your team's strengths.

Starting the Animation Discussion Early in Your Process

Usually, one of the early steps involves discussing the main tasks the app or site is meant to do, or the expected user flows through it. It may sound odd at first, but these early stages are exactly where you want to start talking about animation: Where could it play a helpful role in improving the user experience? Where could it help tell the current story? The earlier in the process animation comes up, the greater the chances that it will be purposeful and make it to the final product.

Design is sometimes written off as "just decoration" by some colleagues or stakeholders, which is always a bit sad for designers. At some point in your career, you've probably fought for the importance of design in a project because you know that design is so much more than just decoration. Purposeful animation needs to be fought for in the same way.

Bringing up animation early in the process goes a long way toward educating stakeholders and team members on how valuable it can be to the overall experience. In addition to that, the earlier you start thinking about ways to incorporate animation into a project, the more time you'll have to iterate on and improve the animated interactions without it seeming like an extra burden of work. Starting early is a win-win for all involved.

Identifying Where Animation Could Be Most Helpful

To evaluate where animation could be most helpful in your project, it helps to focus on a few key questions. When you have identified the major tasks and user flows ask yourself: Could any of the major tasks benefit from additional mechanisms for feedback, focus, causality, demonstration, or orientation?

What is the most important interaction of your site or app? The one thing that offers the most value to your users? This is another good place to start by thinking about where animation could add to the experience. Look at it step-by-step to identify where animation could make the interaction easier, more clear, or better align with your brand's personality. Once you've found a place for animation in that hero interaction, you can use similar patterns throughout the rest of your application for a cohesive sense of motion design across the entire experience.

For example, if your main interaction involves filling out a complex form one step at a time, animating each step in from the left, then out to the right when it's completed, could aid users in keeping track of where they are in the process. Based on this, you might decide to use animation primarily for entrances and exits of content throughout the rest of the application.

Sketching and Storyboarding Animation Ideas

Storyboards are most useful for sketching out and discussing where there is potential to use animation in your designs at the beginning stages of your process. Storyboards can take many different forms, and you may already be using other kinds of storyboards in your design process to examine things like user flows or user stories (see Figure 10.1). This storyboarding step is a perfect place to start thinking and talking about where animation could be employed to improve the user experience.

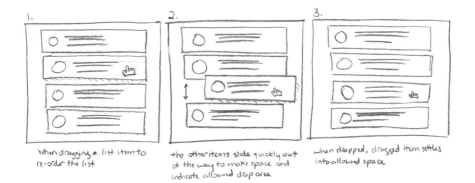

1. When dragging a list item to re-order the list

2. the other items slide quickly out of the way to make space and indicate allowed drop area

3. when dropped, dragged item settles into allowed space

FIGURE 10.1

An example of an early sketched storyboard. It's nothing fancy, but it gets the idea across and can be a great discussion aid.

> **TIP WHAT IS A STORYBOARD?**
>
> For interface animation purposes, storyboards are representa-
> tions of each key stage of an animation, or group of animations,
> drawn frame by frame. Each frame represents a snapshot of what
> will be happening on-screen at a specific point in time in the ani-
> mation. Often, these are sketched out by hand, but they can also
> be created digitally from wireframe or mock-up assets.

More detailed storyboarding may be helpful to examine the flow of specific animated interactions. Sketching out the beginning, end, and middle states of a proposed animation can help you and your team judge its merits at an early stage. You can try out a number of anima-tion possibilities quickly before investing too much time into any one option.

> **TIP STORYBOARDS FOR DOCUMENTATION**
>
> If you're using your storyboards for internal documentation, be
> sure to number each frame and include short descriptions of
> what each frame depicts.

You may have seen some of the gorgeous and detailed storyboards that studios like Pixar use for their early movie development. Those are incredibly beautiful works of art on their own, but luckily, you don't need to create storyboards on that level for animated interactions.

Storyboards don't have to be beautiful works of art to be effective (see Figure 10.2). There's no prerequisite of being a skilled illustrator to use storyboards in your work. Even a roughly drawn storyboard on a white board can save time in meetings by presenting a shared visual document of what's being discussed for everyone to participate. The fast and messy nature of hand-drawn storyboards can show that the idea is still open for input and development. That is a great advantage when you're trying to find the best potential solution for animated interactions and want as much input from your team as possible.

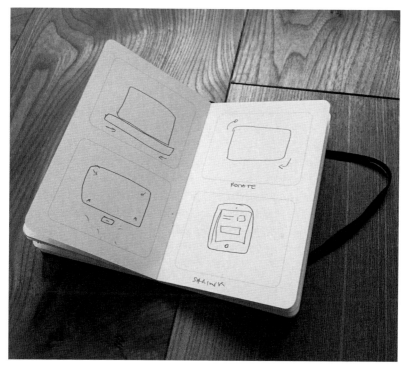

FIGURE 10.2
Chris Gannon creates lovely intricate SVG animations in his work, but even the most complex animations start as rough storyboards like the one above. (Check out **gannon.tv** to see some of Chris's work.)

The Purpose of Storyboards

The two main functions of storyboards for UI animation are:

- A shared visual representation of what is being discussed and its context

- A guide for building the next iteration of the animations

Storyboards are most useful for interface animation when they cover the entire phrase of interaction or user flow. (Refer to the sketched example in Figure 10.1 that covers the entire drag-and-drop action.) That way, they can play a role in identifying where animation can help users achieve their main goals. In the early stages, your main focus should be on finding the places where purposeful animation will improve the experience and define exactly what the purpose is of each animation. No UI animation should make it to the final product without knowing its purpose.

The more traditional way of using storyboards—to diagram the key frames of action in a long-form animation—can also be useful for interface animation. When creating longer running animations that aren't interactive, storyboards can act as a guide for the assets, goals, and content of the animation. In these cases, something a little more polished than just rough sketches may be in order, and you'll likely go through many iterations of your storyboard. Putting the time into defining a solid storyboard on paper will save you time in designing and developing the animation.

Typically, storyboards are used only as internal deliverables: something shared with your team or across different teams within your organization. They're often less useful outside of a presentation or discussion to support and explain them. The main exception to this is when you're working on a long-playing animation where the storyboard is used as a shot list and guide for what assets need to be drawn or created.

When to Use Storyboards

Storyboards are best at answering questions like: Would animation be helpful here? They are most helpful when the details and flow of interactions are still being determined, or when speed and creating a variety of options are more important than fine detail. Storyboards also help answer the question of what order animated interactions

Using Musical Notation to Note Timing Ideas

If you have timing ideas for your animations early on and don't want to forget them, note the rhythm with musical notation in your sketches (see Figure 10.3). I find this to be a huge help in planning out animations myself. It's a great way to put all those childhood piano lessons to use.

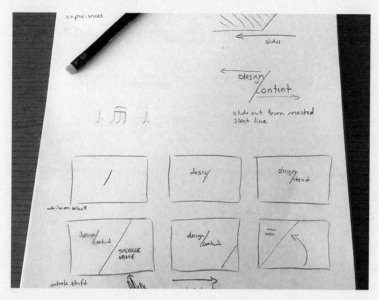

FIGURE 10.3
An example of rhythm notation in rough storyboard sketches.

should happen in or which animations may happen at the same time. The sketching phase or wireframing phase of a project is a perfect place for storyboarding specific animated-interaction ideas.

If you're working on a longer playing storytelling animation—one that is intended to be watched more like a video—then your storyboarding goals change slightly. For this kind of animation, storyboards take on their more traditional use of listing the important frames of the action in order. These will then be used as a guide to determine which assets need to be created, what the timing is of the main points, and how the story will be told. In this case, your storyboard will likely go through many iterations and be used as an ongoing guide while the animation is being authored.

If you use element collages (**danielmall.com/articles/rif -element-collages/**) or style tiles (**styletil.es**) in your design process, you can add a few frames of storyboards in these documents to demonstrate your animation ideas. (This is one of my favorite places to include short storyboards and further the animation conversation.)

Do You Have to Use Storyboards for Interface Animation?

No, storyboards are not a requirement for design interface animations. Some teams love storyboards, some won't go near them, and others fall somewhere in between those two extremes. Many designers only storyboard animation ideas for their own personal sketching or notes and don't share them with anyone else directly. (I tend to be that kind of designer, myself.) How you use them, or if you use them at all, depends on how helpful they are to you. If they're not helping, there's no point in forcing yourself to use them!

Storyboards are meant to aid in the discussion of animation and animation decisions early in the design process. If you're able to have those discussions without them, you're still on your way to creating meaningful animation.

Software to Use for Storyboards

Storyboards are static deliverables, usually shown printed on paper, in a PDF, or maybe even drawn on a whiteboard. If hand-drawing storyboards isn't your style, try drawing your storyboard frames in one of the following:

- Illustrator
- Keynote
- Sketch
- Photoshop

Create Animation Prototypes

Somewhere near the middle of your design process, after you've identified where animation could be useful but you still need to determine the look and feel of that animation, prototyping your animation ideas will be a useful task. In fact, if there's one step not to skip, it's prototyping. Seeing your animation ideas in motion is invaluable for evaluating and improving them.

Animation prototypes differ from storyboards in that they are higher fidelity and they delve into the specifics of what the animations will look like and how they will behave. Animation prototypes can be created with specific prototyping software or coded by hand. They show the appropriate context—reflecting a mobile device for apps or a browser for web projects—and are often also interactive. We'll discuss the various kinds of prototypes and how to create them in detail in the next chapter. Prototyping is a big enough deal to get its own chapter.

TIP PROTOTYPES ARE GREAT FOR GETTING BUY-IN!

Animation mock-ups or prototypes can be the most effective way to get stakeholder buy-in on your animation ideas. Seeing it in action is often much more effective for showing the effectiveness of an interactive animation than a storyboard or verbal description.

When to Use Animation Prototypes

Making animation prototypes often comes after making storyboards, or you might even skip directly to prototyping—especially if the main interactions and flow of tasks are already established and known. There's nothing wrong with skipping straight to prototyping if that's what feels right for your process.

The main question that animation prototypes help answer is: How will this behave? When you're creating prototypes, you take a deeper look at how animations can inform the interaction at hand and start getting into details, like what action triggers an animation, how the animation will be timed, how one object on-screen may influence another, and what each individual animation might look like. Prototypes can even be used in early user testing if you'd like.

Prototypes can be useful at many stages of the design process. High-fidelity prototypes are generally reserved for when the final, or near final, visual design has been completed. They can be used as a way for designers to communicate the details of the animation to the developers who will be building it. On the other hand, lower fidelity prototypes can be used as early as the wireframing stages, especially when you aren't finding storyboards are enough to get your ideas across.

Be an Undercover Animation Hero

One of the questions I get most often after talks or workshops is how to get your boss, client, or teammates to see the value of animation as a design tool. Sometimes, it can feel like you're the only one on your team trying to add purposeful animation into your work.

As wonderful as it would be to change their minds overnight, slow and steady is the most effective option here. The best solution I've found for this is to be an undercover animation hero: to be an internal champion of animation and what it can add to your design efforts at every opportunity.

Start by sharing articles or examples you find online that highlight animation being used effectively. When you encounter examples of well-used motion in your favorite apps or sites, share that with your colleagues or boss as well. (Maybe even share this book with them.)

Keep an eye on your competition's sites and products and see where they are using animation. Make a case for how you could use animation more effectively in your company's work. It may sound cliché, but appealing to their sense of competition can be a highly effective motivator!

Don't wait for permission to include storyboards or motion prototypes in your design deliverables. Include storyboards with your design explorations or element collages. Prepare a motion comp to show how an interaction should animate along with your static comps. Often, these take only a small amount of extra time on your part, but speak volumes when it comes to demonstrating how animation can improve the experience to the rest of your team.

Animation in Your Style Guide

Documenting your animation design decisions into your design documentation or a style guide is a smart way to save yourself from repeating efforts unnecessarily in the future. Once you've gotten a handle on when and where you're using animation in the design of your product or project, documenting your decisions is the logical next step. The goal is to have these decisions, and their supporting logic, documented for your colleagues, clients, or even you. It's important for whomever might be responsible for updating or adding design elements as the project or product matures.

Style guides or design guideline documents are a great place to document your animation design decisions. Many teams already have these documents in place, which makes it even easier to add to them. If you're using similar documentation in your team already, this might be a good excuse to start. Having your team's animation design decisions documented and easy to access means there's a greater chance of having a cohesive experience for your users.

It's important to define your audience for your documentation early. If it's primarily aimed at developers, code samples and best practices for coding animation would be helpful to include. On the other hand, if the main audience is marketing or a PR staff without a strong design background, the focus would need to be on the design reasoning behind the animation and being clear on which elements may or may not be animated. Keeping your audience in mind makes it easier to document just the parts that are most useful and necessary. You want to be sure that the effort that goes into creating the documentation isn't significantly greater than the benefit seen from it. In general, the bigger the audience, the more detailed the documentation needs to be.

There is no one-size-fits-all way of documenting your design decisions, for animation or otherwise. What follows are suggested areas that are most useful to use as a guide while creating documentation that best fits the way your team works.

> **TIP** **MORE ON STYLE GUIDES**
>
> For more on how to create a style guide and what makes a good one, check out the many resources at **styleguides.io**.

Why Document Animation?

Documentation doesn't always sound like the most fun task you could do, but when done well, it can be immensely useful and have noticeable time-saving benefits.

The time-saving benefits of documenting your animation design decisions will be noticeable anytime you have to add functionality or new pages to your project. You won't have to waste time going back into previous designs or code to remind yourself what animation patterns and styles already exist.

Documenting your animations gives you a central place to identify reusable design patterns and code. It will make it easier to share and reuse resources, reuse animations, and make consistent design decisions when it comes to animation. Documentation also helps ensure that all the developers on a team are making consistent decisions on the building blocks of animation, like easing functions, animation keyframes, and variables.

Document the Types of Animation You Use

Documenting the main purposes you use animation for is key to keeping a cohesive motion experience across many pages or screens that your users may encounter. Some of those purposes could be:

- Entrances and exits
- Causality
- Emphasis
- Feedback
- Transitions between states
- Orientation
- Personality and branding
- Storytelling

In earlier chapters, we discussed how to create cohesive choreography across all the animations in a particular project or product. Objects with similar content or intention also have similar animation applied to them to reinforce their similarities. Documenting the main categories of animation can be applied to your designs to highlight these decisions and carry them forward as the design matures.

For example, your style guide may specify that entrances and exits for all objects that come on and off the screen will be animated, and that animation will be handled via specific timing and easing guidelines. Documenting which categories of animation your design employs and why will lay the foundation for consistent motion design decisions moving forward.

Document Your Building Blocks

Take note of what the core building blocks of your animations are and add these to your documentation as well. The main properties of any on-screen object that can be animated are:

- Opacity
- Scale
- Color
- Depth

- Position
- Rotation
- Blur

A single object rarely has all of these properties animated on it at once. Things would get a little crazy if that were the case! You may have chosen to stick to only opacity and scale animation in various combinations in your design. Or perhaps your design relied more on animating depth and position to keep your users oriented in a layered interface. Be sure to document whichever building blocks you used most frequently and why (see Figure 10.4). Some tools like Pattern Lab already have placeholders for some basic animation building blocks built in.[1]

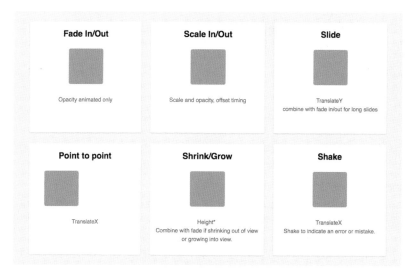

FIGURE 10.4

An example of documented animation building blocks from Shopify's internal motion style guide.

---

1 Pattern Lab demo site: http://demo.patternlab.io/.

Document How You Use Layers and Space

If your interface employs layers for different kinds of content, some above or below others in 3D space (or implied 3D space), you should document where those layers are in relation to each other. For example, if your alert messages are always one layer above your content, you'll want to document this so that any transitions to and from the alerts follow that model consistently.

When your animations respect the different layer depths you've established in your design, it's easier for your audience to create their own mental modal of how those layers related to each other in the space of the interface.

If you have layers in your interface, your documentation should include a diagram of which depths are used for what. How far down or up does each item start? And where does it end up? See Figure 10.5 for an example of how different depth could be documented.

Admin Interface Layers

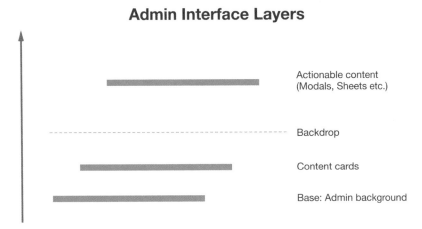

FIGURE 10.5
An example of documenting depth and layers of a particular interface in a motion style guide.

Document How You Employ the Classic Principles

The classic principles give you a shared vocabulary to discuss animation, and that vocabulary can be reflected in your documentation as well.

Is squash and stretch off limits? Do you use follow-through on all your exits and entrance animations? If so, how much does each overshoot its destination? Asking and answering detailed questions like these will help you describe accurately how you express the personality of your brand or product in motion.

The earlier chapter on classic animation principles talked about how important timing and spacing decisions were to communicate with animation. Deciding on a small library of the types of easing your brand uses and documenting those will go far toward ensuring that the animation in any one user's experience will be cohesive (see Figure 10.6).

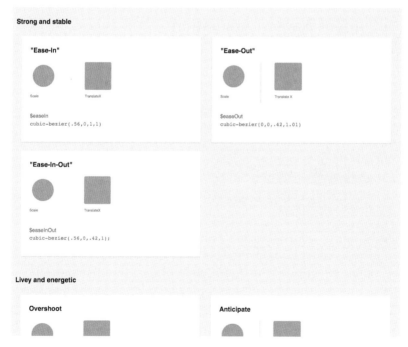

FIGURE 10.6

An example of a portion of an easing palette in a motion style guide. The palette has been grouped by the type of mood or intention that the easings can evoke.

For example, you might determine that variations of Sine easing best express the personality of your product, and therefore you limit the easing functions used in your application to easeOutSine, easeInSine, and easeInOutSine.

Having a system of timing multipliers for your animations can help make them feel like they're operating on a shared sense of rhythm, thus giving a more orchestrated feel to interactions. Your documentation could recommend that all animations' timing be a multiple of 100ms, for example.

Providing some duration presets in your motion style guide can also be helpful. While individual animations may need to have their timing adjusted from time to time, duration presets set out a known starting place or options to try instead of just picking any duration out of your head. A simple set of presets for short, medium, and long animation durations can be enough to offer guidance to whomever is using the style guide to design future animations.

Document Named Animations

As you're designing, you'll most certainly find yourself using a small group of animations over and over. Reusable components are a goal of any design system, and it's no different with animation.

Keep a running list as you're designing or look back on existing designs to identify animations that came up most often and are reused. Also, look for similar animations that could be consolidated into one reusable animation rule instead of two unique ones. One of the hidden benefits of creating style guides is finding unintended variations, which tightens up the consistency and cohesiveness of the overall design system.

Depending on your documentation goals, your documented named animations could be animation building blocks that are meant to be combined—like fade-in, rotate, slide, or something similar. Or they could be groupings of small animations based on the task they complete—like drawer opening, modal window entrance, or something similar.

You can see this distinction in action if you compare the animation section of the Salesforce's Lightning Design System with the animation section of the IBM Design Guidelines. The Lightning Design System (see Figure 10.7) is intended for use by third-party application developers, and it breaks down small building blocks of named animation for developers to use and combine based on their needs.

FIGURE 10.7
Salesforce's Lightning Design System's named animations. They've made their full style guide publicly available at **lightningdesignsystem.com**.

The IBM Design Guidelines,[2] on the other hand, are meant for use by internal IBM teams working on IBM products. Demonstrating cohesive design philosophy and interaction paradigms is the main goal they're trying to accomplish (see Figure 10.8).

No matter what level of detail you choose for them, these named animations can also become the basis of a custom code library for even more time-saving benefits in future design efforts.

---

2 The IBM Design Guidelines: http://www.ibm.com/design/language /framework/animation/introduction.

FIGURE 10.8
The IBM Design Language style guide also includes named animations categorized by function. Each also links to a code and video example of the named animation.

Always Communicate

The biggest factor in designing interface animations well is to keep communicating well. Communication between those responsible for designing the animations and those responsible for building the animations is especially key. Storyboards, prototypes, and documentation are all meant to turn design ideas and decisions into tangible, visual artifacts to keep the conversation going along the way. But don't forget that the conversation itself is the most important part.

Animation needs to be part of the conversation at every step in your design process for the best results.

Creating a motion style guide takes planning and research, but the end result helps save time for future animation efforts and ensures that there's a common feel running through all your animations. The benefits far outweigh the effort it takes to create one, especially for larger teams.

Staying on Point

Keeping animation in mind throughout your entire design process is key to getting the best results. Some helpful ways to ensure that animation is truly a part of your design process:

- Start the animation discussion early.

- Use storyboards to brainstorm animation ideas quickly early on.

- Use prototypes and motion mock-ups to test how your animation ideas hold up to interaction and to discuss ideas with your team.

- Document animation design decisions in your style guide.

- Keep the communication open and discuss animation ideas and opportunities throughout the project life-cycle.

CHAPTER 11

Prototyping Your Animation Ideas

Prototyping is an important part of the design process when you're working with animation. So important, in fact, that it gets its own chapter. Prototypes help you get animation ideas out of your head and onto the screen where you can test them in action, evaluate their behavior, and share them with teammates or stakeholders. There's nothing quite like seeing an animation idea in action. That's what prototypes are so good at.

They are also very effective for communicating and discussing animation ideas with the rest of your team. Prototyping early and often will save you production time and help make sure that everyone involved in designing and building animations is on the same page along the way. In case you can't tell, I really like prototypes.

A third benefit of prototypes is how effective they can be at getting buy-in from stakeholders. Even a quickly made prototype that demonstrates how an interactive animation would work is one of the best ways to get buy-in from the people you need it from, in my experience.

Regardless of the software you choose (and there are so many out there to choose from), there are two factors to measure prototypes by:

- Their level of animation fidelity: That is, how detailed can you get in the control of the animation settings.

- Their level of interactivity: That is, how close can it get to true interactions.

All of the prototyping tools available today, from sketching on paper to specialized software and frameworks, offer varying degrees of both these factors. Smart prototyping means matching the prototype you make to the information you need. Depending on the question at hand, and where you are in your design process, you'll want to see different levels of fidelity and interaction to evaluate your design ideas.

In this chapter, I cover a few different kinds of prototypes from low-fidelity to high-fidelity options. Some of these methods will likely sound more useful to you than others, so feel free to pick and choose which ones will work best for you. There's no requirement to use every prototyping method I mention here; it's all about finding what methods are most effective for you and your team.

Low Fidelity: Sketches and Storyboards

Sketching design ideas as a first step will never go out of style, no matter what you're designing. Even when you're designing things that will be in motion, pencil and paper can still be a great option to work out some initial ideas with simple storyboards. Sketches don't require a computer or software, but they absolutely count as prototypes and are an important first step. These early low-fidelity prototypes are most often sketched quickly on paper as early explorations of the user flow and how animation could be used to support or improve the tasks at hand. They're low fidelity because they don't accurately represent how the animation will look, but that's not important yet in the early stages of deciding what purpose that animation will have.

Low-fidelity prototypes are the quickest to make and the easiest to discard, so they're best used when you want to cover a lot of ideas in a short amount of time. They're also well suited for use at the very start of your design process when goals and ideas may still be a bit fuzzy, and you're still in the conception and sketching phase of your design. Their biggest advantage is how fast they are to create.

Storyboards, paper sketches, or whiteboarding of animation ideas all fall under the category of low-fidelity prototypes (see Figure 11.1). By their nature, these prototypes are also low interaction. You can't click or tap the paper! (But you can describe what happens in response to those interactions in your storyboards or sketches, of course.) The focus is on where and when animation could be placed. The fine-grained details, like exactly what the animation or motion should look like, aren't a primary concern just yet.

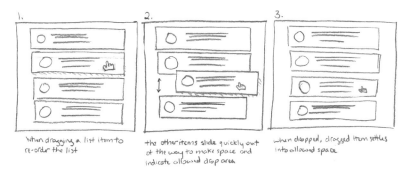

FIGURE 11.1

A low-fidelity sketched storyboard is a great way to prototype your animation ideas early in the process.

Could Animation Be Helpful Here?

Low-fidelity prototypes are best for answering the questions along the lines of: "Could animation be helpful here?" or "Should elements of this interface animate?" or "What order should these tasks happen in?"

When user flows or task flows are still being defined, you should see if animation could help make those flows easier to complete or understand. These prototypes are also good for determining what order complementary animations might happen in, or how specific types of content might behave when animated.

Tools for Low-Fidelity Prototyping

Current tools that I'd recommend for low fidelity prototyping include the following:

- Pencil and paper
- White board
- Illustrator/Sketch (or similar)
- Keynote

Medium to High Fidelity: Motion Comps

Motion comps are short clips of what an animated interaction, or interaction, might look like. (If you've spent any time browsing dribbble.com, you've likely seen a lot of motion comps posted by other designers.) They usually take the form of a video format and are created using visual tools like Keynote, Principle for Mac, Adobe After Effects, or something similar. Chances are you'll pick one of those tools because you're faster at them than building something out in code. One other advantage of using visual tools to build your motion prototype is that they help you focus on the motion without having to dig into the details of how those interface elements will be built.

Motion comps can vary in their degree of animation fidelity, depending on the tool used, but in all cases, they have low interaction ability. (For example, After Effects gives you fine-grained control over all your animation settings, while Keynote has a short list of presets.) They are intended to be watched to demonstrate the desired motion more than to be interacted with. The main purpose of the motion prototype is to demonstrate what the animation will look like and when in the interaction it should occur. The higher animation fidelity your tool of choice can achieve, the more "final" your motion comps will be. Motion comps are great for sharing ideas between designers and developers.

Typically, motion comps start being made around the same time as wireframes are being created and can continue being useful throughout the entire visual design phase of a project. So really, the time to make motion comps is whenever you feel that seeing something in action will be useful. Motion comps may use final design elements or be blocked out with wireframe-like elements, depending on how early in your process you use them. Either approach can be equally effective.

Motion comps usually contain no interactivity. They're more like a movie to show how an interaction or animation could play out, not an actual piece that you can interact with. They may visually simulate clicks or drags for demonstration purposes, though. As such, they tend to show short, linear snippets' task flows—for example, showing what happens when you click on the submit button, but not what happens when you click the cancel button.

How Should These Elements Move On-Screen?

Motion comps are best at answering questions about the behavior of animation: "Does this motion support the interaction at hand?" or "Should these two objects both use animation or just one of them?" or "Does the style of this motion reflect our brand personality?" These kinds of questions tend to be asked on a bigger picture level.

Motion comps are helpful for determining how categories of objects should behave. For example, the call to action buttons should respond to clicks with a color fade animation, while newly introduced content should move onto the screen by sliding in from the left.

Broad global rules for how related objects behave in motion and which types of interactions will use animation can be decided on using motion comps as well. Even though you'll likely only prototype a handful of interactions in animated detail, you can apply the findings from these to the rest of your design work on the project.

Tools for Creating Motion Comps

Current tools that I'd recommend for motion comps prototyping are:

- After Effects (if you're already familiar with it)
- Flash (same as above)
- Atomic.io
- Principle for Mac
- Keynote

Presenting Motion Comps

Motion comps are often shared internally or with clients as a deliverable to demonstrate how interface elements will behave in motion. Often, these will be presented alongside static design mock-ups to fully demonstrate and describe the overall design solution. When presenting in person isn't possible, motion comps might also include a voiceover narration talking through both what the hypothetical user is doing and how the interface is responding. I highly recommend presenting motion comps with a conversation if you'll be sharing them with others. It's so much easier to get the ideas across and receive feedback that way.

Motion comps are also useful to communicate design intentions between designers and developers in a team or across teams. This is one of my favorite ways to use them—communicating to the developer who is building the code. In these cases, a little bit of documentation in addition to discussion of the motion comp will be useful. It gives developers something to refer back to easily if needed and allows designers to document any details that may not be fully covered visually in the prototype itself.

Documenting Animation Detail

At a minimum, any prototype that is being handed off as the final motion to be built should be accompanied with some documentation or explanation of the animation. A video or .gif of an animation doesn't make specifics like the durations or easing choices readily available to the viewer. Anyone expected to re-create these in code will very much appreciate a short note listing those details.

Any prototype you hand off to developers should include:

- The duration of each animation

- The easing equation used for each animation

- Any delay values for the animation

- Any repeat values or iteration counts for the animation

Passing along this information in conversation or chat is completely acceptable, too, if that's how your team prefers to work. As long as the person who's building the animation has easy access to these details, that's documentation enough.

Be sure to document important details like the easing that was used on each element, as well as the durations when handing off motion comps to a developer for a seamless hand-off.

Making a Motion Comp with Keynote

Keynote is a great option for creating low- or medium-fidelity prototypes. It doesn't have robust animation controls like After Effects or some others (which is why it can only do low or medium fidelity), but it can be a big help in getting your motion ideas across. It's software you might have already, and it's easy to use, although you may never have thought of it as a design tool before. Believe it or not, its animation abilities are extensive enough to use it for low- to medium-fidelity prototypes, especially thanks to the "magic move" effect option. Here are the basics of creating a motion prototype in Keynote:

Step 1: Set up your document.

Create a new Keynote file with a basic theme and set custom slide dimensions for the document. I'm mocking up a potential animation for a log-in and registration form that will only take up part of a screen, so a 650px by 600px document size will be more than enough space.

It's also helpful to set the slideshow to loop in the document settings. This allows you to play through your prototype multiple times without relaunching the slide show.

Step 2: Create slides for your "timeline."

The slides of the keynote presentation act as the timeline for the prototype. Each slide is a new state of the animation that Keynote can animate between, using its "Magic Move" feature. You can also create smaller animations within each slide using the various "appear" effects Keynote offers.

For this example, I laid out the wireframed log-in form, which will be the initial state of the form on the first slide (see Figure 11.2). I also created the second state of the form, the registration view, as a grouped element positioned slightly "off-screen" of this slide. (You can grab a premade set of Keynote wireframe elements on Keynotopia.com to make prototyping in Keynote go even faster.)

continues on next page

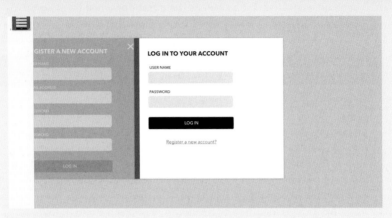

FIGURE 11.2
The first slide of the Keynote prototype with the registration form positioned off-screen.

I duplicated this slide to create the second state of the form that I'll be animating to. All the same elements will be in both states of the form, just in different locations. On the second slide, I moved the registration form from off-screen to its open position covering up the log-in form, as shown below in Figure 11.3.

FIGURE 11.3
The second slide of the Keynote prototype with the registration form fully in view.

Step 3: Animate between slide states.

With these two slides created, I've got the two states of my prototype ready: the closed registration form state and the open registration form state. With both slides selected, the Animate properties tab will let me define how I want to animate between the two.

I selected the Magic Move effect for this animation because I'm moving the registration form into an on-screen position from its initial off-screen starting point (see Figure 11.4). I set a duration of 0.30 seconds with "Ease Out" for the easing and set the animation to occur on click. (The alternative is to trigger the animation automatically, which can also be useful for prototypes that you'd rather have play from start to finish like a video.)

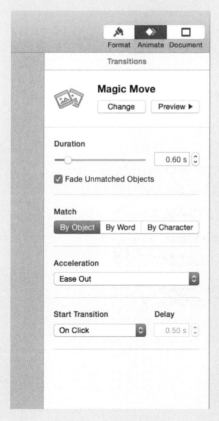

FIGURE 11.4

Keynote's animation menu for the "Magic Move" effect.

continues on next page

Additional items in this prototype could be animated by select-ing various effects for "appearance" in the same Animation menu. Repeat this step until all your desired animations, both between slides and on individual slides, have been created. (You can play the Keynote file at any point along the way to preview your progress.)

Step 4: Playback your prototype.

Playing the Keynote file now will toggle the registration form's animated entrance and exit back and forth on click. It's a quick and simple prototype I can use to demonstrate how the log-in and registration forms should behave (see Figure 11.5).

FIGURE 11.5

The final animated Keynote prototype in action.

High Fidelity: Interactive Prototypes

Interactive prototypes are detailed prototypes built to evaluate the behavior and timing of animated interactions. These are like excerpts of the final product. They are indistinguishable from the final product in terms of their level of interactivity and fidelity of animation, but they are built to represent only one specific task or flow, not the entire product.

Interactive prototypes are created with code-based tools, such as Framer, Origami, or a custom code library, or they are coded from scratch depending on your preference and skill level. They are almost always shown in the native environment of the final product. For example, an interactive prototype of a web app would be shown in a browser, and an interactive prototype for a native app should be shown in a simulator displayed on an appropriate device. Context is important, even at this level of prototyping detail.

Interactive prototypes should be indistinguishable from the final product in terms of behavior. They can be used almost like the real thing. Clicks, drags, hovers and touch events (if applicable) are part of these prototypes. But it's important to note that they don't require actually building out a fully featured product—just one that's good enough to be functional. For example, if you're creating an interactive prototype of an animated form interaction, you might use blank input boxes without full-form validation to get the idea across. The submit button wouldn't do anything besides trigger the submit animation—no actual data would be sent. That form prototype would feel just like interacting with the real thing and would require a fraction of the time of a full build-out of the fully functional form.

When creating a code-based interactive prototype, there may be potential for reusing code from the prototypes in the final product. At the very least, timing functions and easing details, animation timings, or the physics involved in animations could be copied over to the final code base. Even more could be shared across these prototypes and the final product, if desired and planned for. But I wouldn't put too much pressure on creating production-ready code for prototypes. Creating prototypes should be as quick and easy as possible, and the focus should be on the animation portion of it, even if the code behind it is a bit messy.

Interactive prototypes are the place to time and design animations with fine detail and precision. They are the place to experiment and give animations the style and message that best fits their purpose. Easing functions, timing, durations, and offsets timing should be noted for use in the final version.

Does the Animation Feel Right? Is It Usable?

The questions that high-fidelity prototypes are best at answering are ones like "Does this animated interaction feel right to use?" "Is the timing of the animation good?" "Are the animations nonblocking, or do they get in the way of completing the task at hand at any point?"

High-fidelity prototypes are the place to fine-tune your animations before the final product—to decide on your timing, spacing, and other classic principles as they will be reflected in the motion. The option to fine-tune easing and other animation parameters isn't likely to be available in lower fidelity prototyping tools.

Tools for High-Fidelity Prototypes

Current tools that I'd recommend for high fidelity prototyping:

- Framer.js

- Principle

- GreenSock JavaScript Animation Library

- HTML and CSS and JS

Essentially, any prototyping software that lets you create both realistic, usable interactions and gives full control over the animation settings can create high-fidelity prototypes.

Quick Web Prototypes with Screenshots and CodePen

You can make interactive prototypes for the web quickly by combining screenshots of static mock-ups with animated interactive elements layered on top. This is an especially useful method when you're exploring ideas for small sections of animation on a larger page like buttons, modals, or similar objects. This technique gets you to an interactive prototype with a fraction of the effort required to create a full prototype. You can make these as stand-alone HTML pages as well, but making them on a code sharing site like CodePen gets you up and running even faster and makes your prototypes even easier to share. (You can make your prototype private on many of these sites as well to keep them out of the public eye.)

Step 1: To start, take a screenshot of the base screen design from a static mock-up, or a current live page you'll be adding to, and set it as a background image for your page (see Figure 11.6).

(You'll want to hide any of the parts you'll be animating when you take this screenshot so that you can layer them in over the top of it and animate them.)

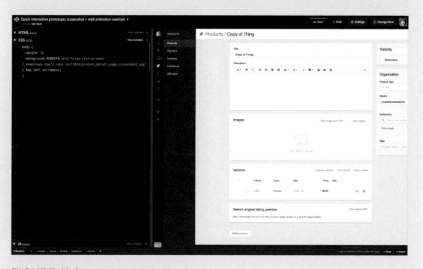

FIGURE 11.6

A CodePen pen with the background image of the prototype in place.

continues on next page

Step 2: Overlay the content you'll be animating for the prototype and position it on the page in the appropriate place.

For this particular prototype, I positioned a button element that will trigger the modal animation over the top of the matching text in the image to make it clickable (see Figure 11.7).

Don't worry about using "hacky" feeling layout shortcuts to get things into place. These prototypes are purely about how the object animates and behaves. The rest of the code won't be production code, so it's allowed to be messy. Think of it like sketching in code. It can be cleaned up for production once you've got the animation finalized.

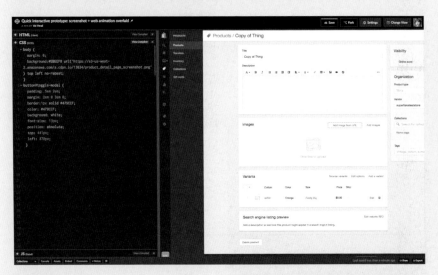

FIGURE 11.7

The updated pen with the active button added and positioned on top of the screenshot background image.

Step 3: Add the interaction and animation behavior for the animated objects.

In this case, I'm animating the modal box into view when the button I created is clicked (see Figure 11.8). Everything else in the prototype besides that button and the modal are just part of the background image. The end result looks a whole lot more real than it really is. The realistic background image gives the prototype the right context without a lot of extra work.

FIGURE 11.8

The final interactive prototype with the modal box animating in when the button is clicked.

How Many Prototyping Tools Should You Use?

Sometimes it seems like there are about a million prototyping tools on the market, but you don't need to be proficient in all, or even most, of them! In fact, despite the wide range of products on the market, you really only need one or two to meet your prototyping needs. The fact that there are so many prototyping tools on the market just means that you have a wide variety to select your favorites from.

I recommend having two prototyping tools in your toolbox: one for low-fidelity prototypes and one for high-fidelity interactive prototypes.

Whatever you choose for your low-fidelity prototypes should be something you can work very quickly in and create prototypes without sinking in a lot of time. It could be something like sketching storyboards or Keynote, or any tool that let's you plan out animation ideas quickly without having to define a lot of the motion detail.

Your chosen tool for high-fidelity prototypes should be one you put a little more time into learning. It should be something you can create prototypes in that look and feel almost exactly like the final product. Framer.js is a good option for creating high-fidelity prototypes in code, as is creating your own custom starter files for a customized toolset. Visual tools for high-fidelity prototypes could be something like Principle or After Effects, which allow you to have precise control over your animation with custom motion curves.

Your high-fidelity tool might be one you use to make motion comps or one you use to make interactive prototypes, depending on how you and your team work. The main goal is to have a tool you can use to reflect the final or near-final easing and timing choices for your animation work.

Remember that prototyping gets easier with time. No matter what tool or method you choose the first time around, making a prototype could take a lot of time. But by the third or fourth time, it will be a breeze.

Prototyping Web Animation in RWD

When you're creating prototypes for the web, you have to keep responsive web design in mind. The behavior of any animations that take up a large amount of screen space or animations that change the position of interface elements can be impacted by a change in viewport size. Solving how these animations should behave at different viewport sizes should be addressed at the prototyping stage. Tackling the viewport size question in prototypes will save you time and potential headaches later on in the process. In general, there are two approaches to prototyping responsively.

Prototyping in Two Sizes

One approach is to prototype the two extremes: how the animation should work on large viewports and on the smallest viewports. Then fill in the in-between viewport sizes during production. The behavior for the in-between viewport sizes can also be addressed in additional documentation.

This approach works best in cases where animated interface items reflow or change positions or dimensions, depending on the size of the viewport. It also works well if you're already using a similar approach to design your static mock-ups. If your team is already accustomed to approaching designs this way, thinking of animation in the same terms can take advantage of that same internal mental model.

Creating Responsive Prototypes

Another approach is to make your prototype itself responsive: to make it "squishy" and fully functional at all viewport sizes. This approach only works for code-based prototypes that can be viewed directly in the browser. It would likely be more trouble than it's worth to try and mimic the browser resizing in another tool.

Highly involved animations, or highly animated interactions, are the best candidates for this approach. This approach works very well for SVG-based animations, too—especially ones that take up a large amount of screen space. The fact that SVGs are vector objects and can be scripted directly makes them a perfect candidate for this. Of course, media query adjustments can be made for both CSS and JavaScript-based animations acting on HTML elements as well.

Keep in mind that not all interface animations need to be adjusted for changing viewport sizes. Animations that affect nonmovement properties like opacity, blurs, color, or similar ones will be just as effective even if the element they're acting upon changes size. For example, an animation that unblurs and flips a button's icon over in 3D space when its hovered over will work the same even if the button has been scaled up or down to fit the available screen space.

How Many Prototypes Should You Make?

There is no magic number of prototypes that every project should aim to make. The different kinds of prototypes mentioned here are a guide to help you determine which kind of prototypes might best fit with the way you currently work. There's no requirement to use them all or even approach them in a specific order.

Your goal should be to prototype just enough to test your assumptions and ideas, and to make the design intention clear. Some teams skip right from initial paper prototypes to building interactive prototypes and rely on lots of communication on their way to the final product. Some teams skip right to the low-fidelity prototypes to test their assumptions and then move to the final product from there.

The key factor I've noticed in every team I've spoken to that does animation well is communication. Regardless of how or how many prototypes they make, they're communicating about both the design and technical goals of what they're working on and how animation fits into those goals.

Some interactions may go through many iterations of prototypes before you arrive at a final version. For others, you might design a great solution after just one round of prototyping. As long as you are learning something from each iteration of a prototype and improving your design choices with each prototype iteration, your prototypes are working for you.

Staying on Point

With all the tools and options available, prototyping can sometimes feel like an overwhelming task. Keep these four points in mind to make your prototyping efforts low stress and focused:

- Quick sketches make for great low-fidelity prototypes to help decide where animation might go and what it might do.

- Motion comps are helpful for planning out specific motion ideas in more detail, focusing on what will animate and how.

- Interactive prototypes help you evaluate the behavior of an animated interaction, how it responds to input, and if it gives timely feedback.

- Interactive prototypes can be quick and simple to make, and they don't have to include fully realized production-ready code.

CHAPTER 12

Animating Responsibly

Every time the topic of animation and accessibility comes up, I remember an accessibility meet-up I attended in 2014. One presenter was a local college student who used a Dynavox system to navigate the web. (He used a customized console of buttons and other controls mounted to the front of his motorized wheelchair.) He was showing us all how he used his college's site with the Dynavox controls. At one point, he arrived at the home page carousel and wanted to click through to the details on one of the stories—a seemingly simple task for many of us. But before he even managed to get to the "Read More" link, the carousel transitioned to the next story, whose "Read More" link was in a different place. Each slide of the carousel moved before he could get his cursor to a link, with no way to pause those slide transitions.

That story sticks with me because it was such a strong reminder that animation design decisions can have a big impact on the end user. It was dramatic and memorable, but it's only one of many ways that animating our interfaces can impact how accessible they are. Sometimes very simple changes or just a little bit of thinking ahead when designing animations can make all the difference as to how accessible they are. Knowing where animation can help the most, choosing the best web animation technology for the job, and designing with progressive enhancement in mind will help you animate responsibly.

Your Brain on Animation

We covered some of the brain benefits of animation in Chapter 1, but it bears repeating here that animation does have potential accessibility benefits. The potential for animation to reduce cognitive load, reduce change blindness, and inform spatial relationships can add up to interfaces that are more accessible for certain groups of people. (Change blindness is a perceptual phenomenon that occurs when a change in a visual stimulus is introduced and the observer doesn't notice it.)

Animation can be used to guide tasks, focus attention through changing the content hierarchy, and give more meaningful feedback as well. All of these benefits can make otherwise complex changes of state or orientation in an interface easier to follow for anyone with reduced cognitive abilities.

But there must be a balance between animation and accessibility, because there is the potential to do good as well as harm. The name of the game is to be well-informed and balance all the factors to make design decisions that work best in the context of your particular project.

Animation and Vestibular Disorders

The idea that animation in our interfaces is capable of making people dizzy or worse wasn't something the web had to contend with until recently. It's actually a fairly new revelation in most tech circles. Even Apple discovered this the hard way when the animated transitions in iOS 7 started making some people sick.[1] Just like other elements of design, the way you use animation can have an impact on how accessible the end product is to your audience.

A Vesti-What Disorder?

Vestibular disorders don't tend to come up very often in web design discussions, so if you haven't heard of them before, you're not alone. Because these disorders are often triggered by movement, they were left out of web accessibility discussions before today's modern web animation landscape existed.

> **NOTE** VESTIBULAR DISORDER DEFINED
>
> The vestibular system includes the parts of your inner ear and brain that process sensory information and control your balance and eye movements. Any disease, damage, or injury to the vestibular system falls under the umbrella of a vestibular disorder. There is a long list of specific vestibular disorders ranging from dizziness and vertigo to more serious conditions.[2]

These disorders can affect people of all ages, and the severity and symptoms vary from individual to individual. Estimating an exact number of people affected by this, let alone what percentage of your specific audience may be affected, can be difficult to pin down. According to vestibular.org, approximately 8 million American adults report a chronic problem with balance, while an additional 2.4 million report a chronic problem with dizziness.

As animated interfaces become more and more the norm, more people have realized that dramatic, large-scale motion on-screen can cause dizziness, nausea, headaches, or worse. For some, the symptoms can last long after the animation is over. Thankfully, you can do something about it.

---

1 Why iOS 7 Is Making Some Users Sick: http://rfld.me/1NaRh9X.

2 Types of Vestibular Disorders: http://rfld.me/1V4n5jx.

To get a better idea of what sorts of web animation are triggers for people with vestibular disorders, I chatted with Greg Tarnoff and Craig Grannell about their experiences. Greg, who experiences vertigo and migraines, is an accessibility and UX consultant, writer, and speaker. Craig, who experiences dizziness, is a writer and editor who has written about the effects of iOS's animations for publications like *The Guardian*. Both of them have been vocal about how interface animations affect people with vestibular disorders.

Greg identified Vimeo's Cameo, Ice and Sky, and RD Construction as troublesome, due to their large areas of motion and the parallax-like effects of background and foreground moving at different speeds (see Figures 12.1 and 12.2).

For Craig, the carousel on Apple.com poses a big problem, especially when it flicks back to the first picture. There are no controls to pause or stop that particular carousel, so there's no way to avoid it.

FIGURE 12.1
The full-screen parallax movement of Ice and Sky proved to be problematic and triggering. You can see it in action here: **https://vimeo.com/164193556**.

The iPhone product page (apple.com/iphone/why-theres-iphone/), with its parallax-ish background animations and scroll-jacking (where the backgrounds animate in at a speed unrelated to your scrolling efforts), causes problems as well.

Craig also describes wired.co.uk's horizontal shift when you scroll to the bottom of the page as "a nasty surprise," if you're not prepared for it. Seeing a huge horizontal shift when you're scrolling downward is certainly a drastic departure from expectations.

For a longer first-person account of what it's like to live with a vestibular disorder, Marissa Christina does a wonderful job of describing what it's like in her interview on *The Big Web Show*.[3] Her site, abledis.com, is full of great insights and information as well. (The section on motion warnings seems defunct now, but a lot of insight can be gleaned from the comments.)

FIGURE 12.2
The full-screen 3D flip with a touch of parallax added in caused problems when viewing the RD Construction site. You can see it in action here: https://vimeo.com/164193557.

---

3 Marissa Christina on *The Big Web Show*: http://rfld.me/1qVoGMn.

Identifying Potentially Triggering Animation

Different people have different conditions and reactions, of course, but the potential triggers are more nuanced than just assuming any or all animation will be problematic. There are three factors in particular that play a big part: the relative size of the animation(s), the direction of movement, and the perceived distance an animated object covers.

Relative Size of Movement

Animations that take up a large amount of space are the most likely culprits to trigger a negative response for someone suffering from a vestibular disorder. The physical size of the screen matters less than the size of the animation relative to the screen space available. So a small form field or button transition probably won't cause trouble, but a full-screen state transition covering the entire screen likely would.

Mismatched Directions of Movement

Exaggerated parallax and scroll-jacking animations are highly likely to be triggering factors. Much of the time, these effects involve background objects moving at a different speed than foreground objects, and sometimes the difference in speed is quite drastic. Animations that move against or in a way that is not directly associated with the speed at which the user is scrolling also tend to be problematic. It's not much of a stretch to see how that could be disorienting.

Distance Covered

The amount of spatial distance covered by an animation is a factor as well. It's virtual space, of course, but animations covering a large perceived distance can trigger a reaction. For example, the iOS 3D zoom transitions that caused people trouble covered a lot of virtual space at a very high rate of speed.[4]

Designing Safer Motion for the Motion Sensitive

Even those who suffer from vestibular disorders themselves rarely want to see all interface animation eliminated everywhere. In fact, some still very much appreciate it from a design perspective. There are a few things you can do to make animation easier on people who find it to be a trigger.

---

4 The Weird, Terrifying Physics of iOS 7: http://rfld.me/1Qa2L8b.

Be Purposeful

We've talked about purpose a lot in this book. Starting your animation decisions from the perspective of purpose helps set you up well for designing accessible animation, too. Starting with thoughtful, purposeful motion sets a good foundation to build upon.

Provide Meaningful Context

A link billed as "the most awesomest spintastic WebGL experiment" likely contains large amounts of animation, and users can make an informed decision as to whether following that link is something they want to do. They can reasonably guess what to expect at the other end of that link and make the call as to whether it's worth the risk to them or not.

Identifying that context gets trickier when motion, even at a large scale, becomes more and more commonplace. When large amounts of animation are part of a news article, for example, the situation changes. With no reasonable expectation of encountering highly animated content, people suffering from a vestibular disorder may find themselves dealing with an onset of symptoms they hadn't expected.

If you aren't certain the context is clear, adding it explicitly could be helpful as well. The A11Y project[5] suggests: "Give an indicator of what movement will happen on the site when a user takes action." Context and setting user expectations is important.

Provide an Option to Reduce Animation

If you do have large amounts of movement that cover a lot of visual ground, consider offering an option to turn off, or reduce, the amount of motion. There are plenty of cases where large amounts of motion make perfectly good design sense. Providing what essentially boils down to an alternative way to view that content, or a little extra control, can be a big help for anyone sensitive to motion.

This can be accomplished via a button or toggle switch to reduce or turn off animation globally on your site. This does take a little more work on your part, but it offers an important option. If it could make the difference between being able to spend time with your content or not, even for a small number of users, it would be worth the effort.

---

5 The A11Y Project: a11yproject.com.

Holohalo.net has an elegant implementation of an animation toggle on its site (see Figure 12.3). An on/off toggle in the top-right corner labeled *animation* defaults to the on position, but it can be toggled off to reduce the amount of animation on the site. The off position stops all the large rotating movements to reduce the triggering potential of the content.

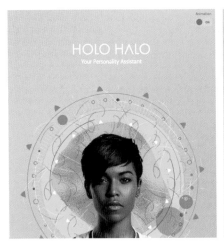 

FIGURE 12.3

The animation toggle switch on **holohalo.net** reduces the amount of animation on-screen when toggled to the off position. You can see it in action here: **https://vimeo.com/164193555**.

A Little Help Here, Browsers?

A toggle solution is better than nothing, but browsers could provide a more universal and easier-to-implement version. Motion-sensitive people often disable Flash or JavaScript at the browser level to help them avoid animation on the web. This may have been somewhat effective in the past (though I doubt it was ever a great solution), but it's definitely not a workable solution on today's web with CSS, SVG, and animated gifs making up a big part of the animation landscape.

Outside of the web, motion-sensitive users of mobile and desktop operating systems are running into similar issues as animation becomes an unavoidable part of the software they use. We're probably going to see a lot more pressure put on OS and browser makers to provide better options for reducing animation.

Animation, Epilepsy, and Migraines

People with vestibular disorders aren't the only ones who can have deleterious effects triggered by animation on-screen. Light, sound, and animation can have an impact on people with epileptic and migraine disorders as well.

Any animation that flashes the screen can be especially risky for anyone with epilepsy. The Web Content Accessibility Guidelines cautions against flashing the screen more than two times a second to avoid triggering seizures. Chances are you're not very likely to be literally flashing the screen in many of your animations. But fast hard cuts from one background color to the next could be perceived as flashes, especially when it takes up a large amount of the screen.

The easiest fix for any flashing you find in your animation is to make sure that change happens less frequently. Or you could try a less jarring transition such as crossfading between background colors instead of a hard cut. If flashing is a necessary part of the effect you're creating, be sure to add a warning for users before they encounter the animation.

Animation and Motor Control

As the story at the beginning of this chapter illustrates, providing controls for any continually updating animation is a huge benefit for those with limited motor control. That means carousels, auto scrolling news updates, or anything similar.

At a minimum, there should be some way to pause these animations and restart them again if desired. Adding a play/pause button could easily take care of this. But a more robust solution could be to have the carousel items automatically pause if they are being interacted with. Giving the user control over when the content advances would also make it easier for anyone with reduced motor control. The W3C offers additional tips specifically for creating accessible carousels here: http://rfld.me/1RWHzYV.

Making sure that any animations that can be interacted with are keyboard accessible is also important. Even if someone isn't able to use a mouse or a similar pointing device, they should still be able to navigate your site. Any animation controls you provide should be able to gain focus and be usable from the keyboard. Test your focus order, especially if you have animated navigation. Be sure that keyboard events and touch events can trigger any necessary callbacks for interacting with animated elements, too. Also make sure that any essential animations still fire via keyboard access.

Carousels specifically might not be your thing, but keep these same guidelines in mind any time you have a part of your interface that both moves on its own and requires interaction.

Animation and Screen Readers

UI animation is purely visual. Anyone using screen readers will miss out on those visual cues, of course. It's important to be sure that missing the animation won't also mean missing critical information.

For things like images and canvas, your best bet is to alternate content in the form of alt tags or a visually hidden description. Write clear descriptive alternate content that conveys the same meaning or intention as best you can. The same goes for an embedded SVG. To a screen reader, that's just an image, and it can't delve inside.

An animated block of text will be read the same way a static one is as long as it is rendered in the DOM when the page loads. So, text that fades into view, or is animated in from a position off-screen, will be read as if it were already there. That's an easy win. If you're injecting new text-based content dynamically as you animate it into view, it will be read by the screen reader only if it has an ARIA live region.

ARIA roles will also come in handy for describing the contents of an inline SVG. SVGs have their own document structure and when they are used inline, screen readers can access these ARIA roles, as well as any live text in the SVG. The flexible scalable nature of SVG is an added bonus for those with low vision. Unlike their raster cousin's canvas, SVGs can be scaled up and zoomed into without losing quality. That's a very much appreciated bonus for anyone with less than 20/20 vision.

The WCAG on Animation

The Web Content Accessibility Guidelines don't say a whole lot about animation, but they do offer up some basic considerations. Following these recommendations will make your design more inclusive, which will have a positive impact for anyone using your site, regardless of any disability. The two animation-focused recommendations they list are:

- Don't flash the screen more than three times a second.

- Add pause controls on animations longer than five seconds.

Pause-and-Play Controls

There are two cases where the WCAG recommends providing pause-and-play controls for animated content. The first is when any moving, blinking, or automatic scrolling lasts for more than five seconds. The second is for any auto-updating content. Looping carousels or notification streams are often auto-updating and should most definitely have some mechanisms to stop and start them as needed.

The five-second rule (this is a different five-second rule than you're used to) is less likely to apply to UI animations. For example, if a state transition or a button hover took five seconds to complete, you'd have bigger problems on your hands. But an animated hero graphic or an animated software demo could easily surpass five seconds. And when they do, make sure that you add some pause-and-play controls.

Screen Flashing Threshold

This isn't something we do often in web animation currently, especially not in the realm of UI animation. But it's an important rule to be aware of. Flashing the screen faster than this three times-a-second threshold has the potential to trigger seizures—even if only a portion of the screen is flashing—so it's not one to be taken lightly.

As you're creating more complex animation that is truly ingrained in your design, be sure to look beyond what is specifically stated in guidelines like the WCAG. Even if your design doesn't include anything specifically cited as an example in the checklist, it might still fall under the descriptions of the guidelines. Whenever in doubt, opt for giving control to the user. Knowing who your design decisions might affect, and how, helps you make better design choices all-around.

For more specifics on techniques and approaches, check out The Accessibility Project (a11yproject.com) or webacessibility.com's best practices for animation as a starting point.

Progressive Enhancement and Animation

As a concept, progressive enhancement balances the desire to use cutting-edge features with the need to not leave out less capable browsers or devices. By using this approach—starting with your base functionality and adding layers of enhancement from there—your design can be universal and push boundaries. The best of both worlds! Choosing to use the latest and greatest web animation capabilities won't mean shutting out anyone in your potential audience, due to lack of browser or device support.

TIP PROGRESSIVE ENHANCEMENT EXPLAINED

One of my favorite explanations of progressive enhancement is in this "24 Ways" article by Jeremy Keith: **https://24ways.org/2014/responsive-enhancement/**.

On the web, you have no control over what environment your work will be viewed in, but you do have control over how your work is built. You can build it in a way that can adapt as needed to nearly any environment you throw at it.

There are two factors to getting progressive enhancement right according to Jeremy Keith: setting up the core functionality and layering up enhanced features as they are supported. It's important to remember that enhancement doesn't mean extra or fluff. The enhancements you create for more capable browsers are just as important as the base functionality. They offer additional features and accommodations and are an important part of the final product.

Progressive enhancement is often framed as a question of what happens when someone visits your site with JavaScript turned off, or if JavaScript becomes unavailable. Even though web animation isn't always done with JavaScript alone, thinking of animation as a layer of enhancement helps make sure that nothing will break or become unusable if your animations (built in JavaScript, CSS, or anything else) can't be viewed.

The Core Functionality for Animation

The core functionality for any animated elements is usually tied to basic DOM elements at their base. When you're animating DOM elements, your goal should be to code those elements using semantic, meaningful HTML markup. Lists should be <li>s even if they're animated, and links should be anchors. Animated text should be marked up as titles or paragraphs at the base level. That kind of thing. When the base content of what you're animating can still be understood even if all the CSS and JavaScript didn't load, you've set up a good starting place.

There will be times when you might need to add additional containers or wrappers to create the animation effects you want, but that's OK. This comes up a lot especially with CSS animation because of the difficulty of combining unique animations on different transform properties of the same element. A few extra wrappers or containers won't hinder the usefulness of your base elements.

TIP PROGRESSIVE ENHANCEMENT IN DETAIL

For a detailed look at progressive enhancement and how to pull it off in a variety of contexts, check out "Adaptive Web Design" by Aaron Gustafson: **adaptivewebdesign.info**.

Experiments and Responsibility

All of these approaches are perfectly doable when the core of what you're designing is a document, as many things on the web are. The web was all started to share documents after all. They're in its blood. But not everything on the web is a document. Not everything you can view in a browser *has* to be a document.

The browser window can be a stage, or it can be a place to watch a film, or it can be a place to play games. I'm sure there are plenty of other exciting things you will be able to do with browsers in the future that I haven't thought of yet. I find that especially exciting.

When you're pushing the limits of the web to bend it to your imagination, you might have to compromise on being as responsible as you'd like. The functionality to make something accessible sometimes lags behind the cutting edge. (Take the <video> element, for example.) If there really is no practical way you can make your experiment and have it be fully accessible, do what you can and give proper warning of anything that might be harmful, but follow your dreams and make something amazing.

I'd rather see you push boundaries and push for what you want the web to be able to do in the future than be held back by what it's only capable of doing today.

Layering in Animation as Enhancements

With that solid base of meaningful mark-up in place, you can start adding in animation as one of your layers of enhancement, loading in the CSS and/or JavaScript that handles your web animations for browsers that are capable of displaying it.

When layering in your Web animation like this, it can be very helpful to have the beginning and end states of any animation handled in the same place. For example, an object that is positioned off-screen initially as part of the layout so that it can be animated into view later, would never be seen if the animation-related code weren't loaded. A more fault-tolerant way of handling this would be to load in both the mark-up that moves the object off-screen and the mark-up that animates it into view at the same time as part of your layer of animation enhancement.

Considering the accessibility impact of your animation work and building in web animation as an enhancement helps ensure that your work can be used and viewed comfortably by as many people and devices as possible. It helps make your work more future-proof as well. Those are all good things!

Staying on Point

When you're trying to create accessible, progressively enhanced web animation, keep the following points in mind:

- Animation has the potential to be both beneficial and harmful for accessibility. Aim to minimize the harmful potential while maximizing the potential benefits.

- You can design safer motion for those with vestibular disorders by being purposeful with your animation, offering accurate context cues, and providing an option to reduce motion, if needed.

- Treat animation as a layer of enhancement that helps make your work more universal and less fragile.

CONCLUSION

This Is Just the Beginning

I hope you've enjoyed this journey into the UX and design side of interface animation. It's an exciting and challenging world to be getting into, especially on the web.

No other medium but the web has the potential to create animation that is accessible, responsive, and progressively enhanced all at the same time. That kind of power can be both exciting and overwhelming, or maybe even a little of both. There is a lot of opportunity and potential for creativity in the future of web animation as it matures and its capabilities expand.

Thinking about animation as a design tool and finding that balance of purpose and style for your animation work can be challenging at times, but with some time and practice, I know you'll make great work with it. Keep on animating, think big, and go make amazing things that redefine what animation can be on the web.

INDEX

H

Halas, John
  Timing of Animation, 19, 40
high-fidelity prototypes, 185–186
Holo Halo, 202
Hootsuite, 129
HTML and CSS and JS tools, 186
HTML markup, 207

I

IBM Design Guidelines, 171–172
IBM Machines in Motion, 149–150
Illusion of Life, The (Disney's Animation), 16–18, 34, 40
Illustrator, 162
interactions, context changes in, 75–77
interactive prototypes, 184–185
iOS update, affordance hint example, 97
iPhone lock screen, 97
Irish, Paul, 56

J

JavaScript, 206
Johnston, Ollie, 16, 34, 40

K

Keith, Jeremy, 206
Keynote software, 143
  motion comp creation, 181–184
  motion comp tools, 179
  storyboard software, 162

L

Lasseter, John
  The Principles of Animation, 40
layers
  animation movement between, 67
  documenting in design process, 168
  as enhancement, 208
  Leapsecond2015 site example, 65–67
  Shopify site sign-up modal example, 64–65
  splitting interface into, 64
  Wacom site navigation layers, 62–63
Leapsecond2015 site, 65–67
Lewis, Paul, 56
linear easing, 21
loader animations
  contextually fit, 120–121
  feedback mechanisms, 118–121
low-fidelity prototypes, 177–178

M

MailChimp, 126–127
Mammoth Booth, 49–50
Marked interface, 130–131
Medium contextual content, 100–101
medium- to high-fidelity prototypes, 178–184
mental models, 62
Messenger app (Facebook), 75
migraines, 203
mismatched motion, 10, 200
Mitchell, Rusty
  The Psychology of Waiting, Loading Animations, and Facebook
Model Human Processor, 53